How to Use This Book

Look for these special features in this book:

SIDEBARS, **CHARTS**, **GRAPHS**, and original **MAPS** expand your understanding of what's being discussed—and also make useful sources for classroom reports.

FAQs answer common **F**requently **A**sked **Q**uestions about people, places, and things.

WOW FACTORS offer "Who knew?" facts to keep you thinking.

TRAVEL GUIDE gives you tips on exploring the state—either in person or right from your chair!

PROJECT ROOM provides fun ideas for school assignments and incredible research projects. Plus, there's a guide to primary sources—what they are and how to cite them.

Please note: All statistics are as up-to-date as possible at the time of publication.

Consultants: William Loren Katz; John Madsen, Department of Geological Sciences, University of Delaware; Jonathan Russ, Professor of History, University of Delaware

Book production by The Design Lab

Library of Congress Cataloging-in-Publication Data
Heinrichs, Ann.
 Delaware / by Ann Heinrichs.
    p. cm.—(America the beautiful. Third series)
 Includes bibliographical references and index.
 ISBN-13: 978-0-531-18597-1
 ISBN-10: 0-531-18597-4
 1. Delaware—Juvenile literature. I. Title. II. Series.
 F164.3.H45 2009
 975.1—dc22   2008000650

AMERICA ★ THE ★ BEAUTIFUL

Delaware

BY ANN HEINRICHS

Third Series

Children's Press®
An Imprint of Scholastic Inc.
New York ★ Toronto ★ London ★ Auckland ★ Sydney
Mexico City ★ New Delhi ★ Hong Kong
Danbury, Connecticut

CONTENTS

GROWTH AND CHANGE

4

A gunpowder mill changes Delaware history, people flee slavery along the Underground Railroad, and small businesses grow into booming industries. **44**

Tenth Street, Wilmington, Del.

MORE MODERN TIMES

5

Delawareans survive the Great Depression and World War II and watch the DuPont Company grow. At the same time, they struggle to gain equal rights for all. . . . **56**

PROJECT ROOM

★

★

9 TRAVEL GUIDE

Explore the First State's shores, shipwrecks, colonial sites, historic buildings, gardens, parks, and museums. **106**

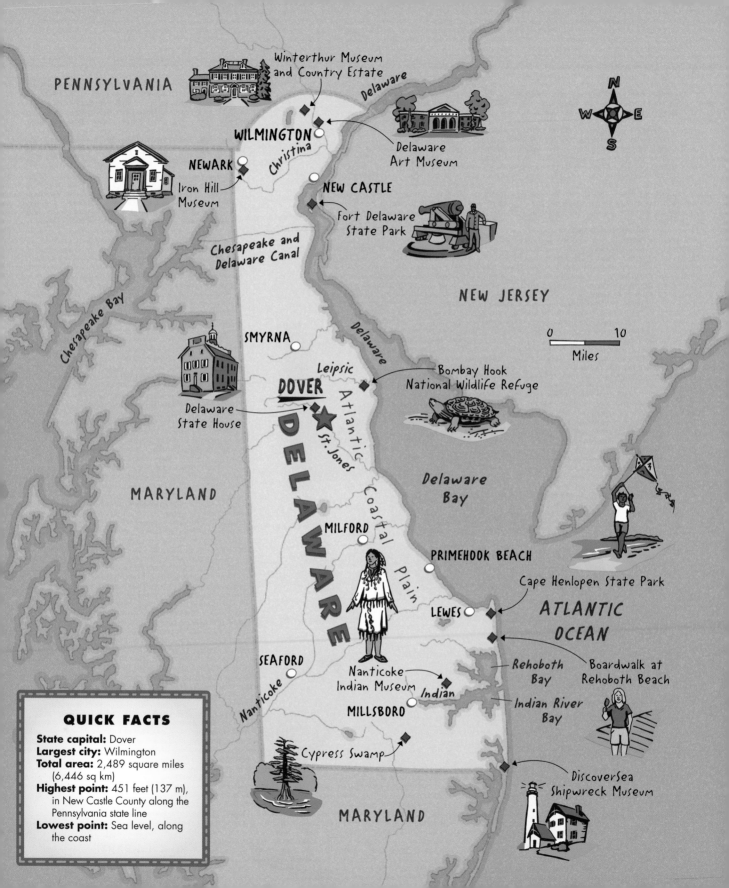

PENNSYLVANIA

Winterthur Museum and Country Estate

Delaware

WILMINGTON

Christina

NEWARK

Iron Hill Museum

Delaware Art Museum

NEW CASTLE

Fort Delaware State Park

Chesapeake and Delaware Canal

Chesapeake Bay

NEW JERSEY

0   10
Miles

SMYRNA

Delaware State House

DOVER

St. Jones

Leipsic

Delaware

Bombay Hook National Wildlife Refuge

Atlantic Coastal Plain

Delaware Bay

MARYLAND

DELAWARE

MILFORD

PRIMEHOOK BEACH

Cape Henlopen State Park

LEWES

ATLANTIC OCEAN

SEAFORD

Nanticoke

Nanticoke Indian Museum

Indian

MILLSBORO

Rehoboth Bay

Boardwalk at Rehoboth Beach

Indian River Bay

Cypress Swamp

DiscoverSea Shipwreck Museum

MARYLAND

QUICK FACTS

State capital: Dover
Largest city: Wilmington
Total area: 2,489 square miles (6,446 sq km)
Highest point: 451 feet (137 m), in New Castle County along the Pennsylvania state line
Lowest point: Sea level, along the coast

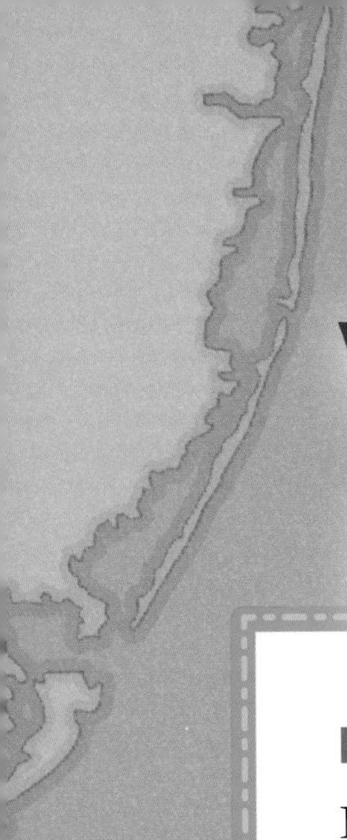

Welcome to Delaware!

HOW DID DELAWARE GET ITS NAME?

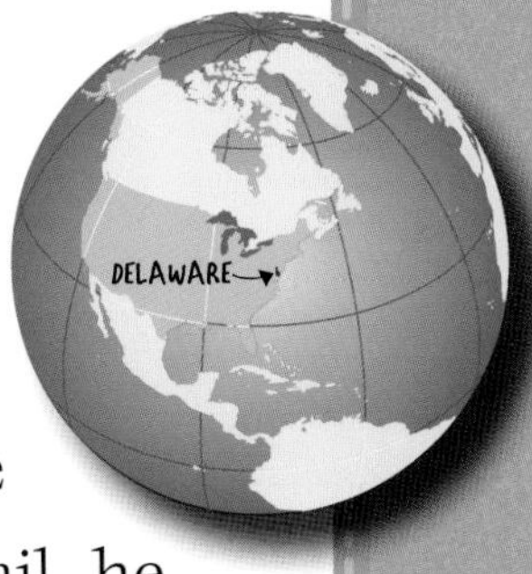

Delaware got its name thanks to a storm. In 1610, an English sea captain named Samuel Argall sailed out from the Virginia coast, south of today's Delaware. He was headed across the Atlantic Ocean to England. Soon after setting sail, he was blown off course in a storm. The winds blew his ship into a body of water unknown to the British. Argall named it De La Warr Bay, in honor of Virginia's governor, Thomas West, Lord De La Warr. That waterway is today's Delaware Bay. Later, people used the name De La Warr, or Delaware, for the river that empties into the bay. They applied the same name to the land on the water's western shore. That land is now the state of Delaware.

DELAWARE→

ATLANTIC
OCEAN

8

READ ABOUT

A view of
Breakwater
Lighthouse at
Cape Henlopen

CHAPTER ONE

LAND

★

DELAWARE IS A VERY SMALL STATE. In fact, only the state of Rhode Island has a smaller land area. Covering 2,489 square miles (6,446 square kilometers), Delaware is mostly low-lying and level. Its lowest point is sea level along the coast, while its highest point is only 451 feet (137 meters) at a spot near the border with Pennsylvania. The state has about 90 miles (145 km) of shoreline along Delaware Bay and about 24 miles (39 km) along the Atlantic Ocean. Sandy beaches, swift-running creeks, and lush natural areas have earned Delaware one of its nicknames: Small Wonder.

The Christina River flows into the Delaware River near the city of Wilmington.

WORD TO KNOW

estuary *the mouth of a river where the river's freshwater mixes with the salt water of the ocean, creating a variety of habitats*

WHERE IS DELAWARE?

Delaware lies along the East Coast of the United States. It occupies the northeastern section of the Delmarva Peninsula. This piece of land is named after the three states that share it—Delaware, Maryland, and Virginia. Maryland lies to the west and south of Delaware. To the north is Pennsylvania. To the east, the Delaware River and Delaware Bay separate the state from New Jersey. The Delaware Bay is an **estuary**, which connects with the Atlantic Ocean. Part of Delaware's eastern coast faces the Atlantic Ocean.

Delaware Topography

Use the color-coded elevation chart to see on the map Delaware's high points (orange) and low points (green to dark green). Elevation is measured as the distance above or below sea level.

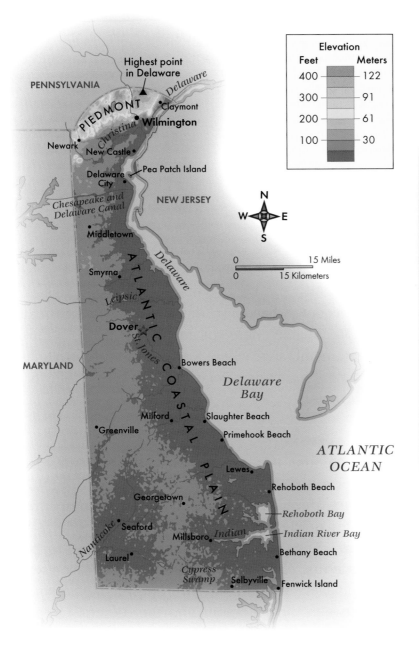

Elevation		
Feet		Meters
400		122
300		91
200		61
100		30

Highest point in Delaware

PENNSYLVANIA

PIEDMONT

Delaware

Claymont

Wilmington

Christina

Newark

New Castle

Delaware City

Pea Patch Island

Chesapeake and Delaware Canal

NEW JERSEY

Middletown

N
W E
S

ATLANTIC COASTAL PLAIN

Smyrna

Leipsic

Delaware

Dover

St. Jones

MARYLAND

Bowers Beach

Delaware Bay

Milford

Slaughter Beach

Greenville

Primehook Beach

ATLANTIC OCEAN

Lewes

Georgetown

Rehoboth Beach

Rehoboth Bay

Seaford

Indian

Millsboro

Indian River Bay

Nanticoke

Laurel

Bethany Beach

Cypress Swamp

Selbyville

Fenwick Island

0   15 Miles
0   15 Kilometers

FAQ

Q: WHAT IS THE WEDGE?

A: The Wedge, or Delaware Wedge, is a tiny notch of land where the borders of Delaware, Pennsylvania, and Maryland meet. When boundaries were drawn in the 1700s, this nearly triangular piece of land was left out. Its ownership was originally claimed by both Delaware and Pennsylvania. The dispute was not settled until 1892, when Delaware was granted the land.

Delaware Geo-Facts

Along with the state's geographical highlights, this chart ranks Delaware's land, water, and total area compared to all other states.

Total area; rank . . . . 2,489 square miles (6,446 sq km); 49th
Land; rank . . . . 1,954 square miles (5,061 sq km); 49th
Water; rank . . . . 536 square miles (1,388 sq km); 40th
Inland water; rank . . . . 72 square miles (186 sq km); 49th
Coastal water; rank . . . . 371 square miles (961 sq km); 15th
Territorial water; rank . . . . . . 93 square miles (241 sq km); 21st
Geographic center . . . Kent County, 11 miles (18 km) south of Dover
Latitude . . . . 38°27' N to 39°50' N
Longitude . . . . 75°2' W to 75°47' W
Highest point . . . . 451 feet (137 m), in New Castle County
along the Pennsylvania state line
Lowest point . . . . Sea level, along the coast
Largest city . . . . Wilmington
Longest river . . . . Delaware River

Source: U.S. Census Bureau

WOW Delaware could fit inside Alaska, the largest state, 266 times!

LAND REGIONS

Delaware has two distinct land regions—the Piedmont and the Atlantic Coastal Plain. These regions were formed by violent upheavals in the earth's crust. Europe, Africa, and the Americas were once joined together as a massive continent. About 200 million years ago, volcanoes began to erupt, cracking this continent apart. Water filled the gap, eventually becoming the Atlantic Ocean. The northwestern section of the ancient continent became North America. As this section drifted west, its cracked edge sank down, becoming the jagged, low-lying Atlantic coast. Meanwhile, more volcanoes near the coast thrust up a mountain range whose tops were worn down to hills over time. Present-day Delaware's landscape reflects all these events.

The Piedmont

The Piedmont is a hilly region that stretches from New Jersey in the north to Alabama in the south. In Delaware, the hills and valleys of the Piedmont cover the state's northern tip, or about 10 percent of the state's land area. The Piedmont is composed of **metamorphic** and **igneous** rock related to continental collision when the Appalachian Mountains were formed. The boundary between the Piedmont and the Atlantic Ocean is known as the Fall Zone. There are many rocks in the

WORDS TO KNOW

metamorphic *describing rocks that have been changed by extreme pressure, wind, and water*

igneous *describing rocks that have been created by magma and volcanic activity*

This soybean field is in Sussex County, which is found in the Atlantic Coastal Plain.

streams that flow between the two regions. Many large cities along the Atlantic Coast are located at the Fall Zone because that was as far as sailing ships could travel inland. People settled where the ships stopped.

The Atlantic Coastal Plain

Some 90 percent of Delaware lies in the Atlantic Coastal Plain. This region—which was once the cracked edge of a splitting continent—runs along the Atlantic Ocean from New Jersey to Georgia. In Delaware, this low, level plain barely rises higher than 60 feet (18 m) above sea level. Much of inland Delaware is farmland. Dover, the capital city, is in this region, about halfway between the Piedmont and the Atlantic Ocean.

At the southern border of Delaware, the Atlantic Coastal Plain contains a wetland called Cypress Swamp. On hiking trails through this dark, moist forest, you'll see herons wading in shallow water and turtles sunning themselves on logs.

RIVERS AND COASTS

The Delaware River is the state's largest river. Most of the state's streams, often called creeks, are small. Brandywine Creek (also known as Brandywine River) crosses northern Delaware and flows through Wilmington, Delaware's largest city. Much of the state's early industry grew up along the Brandywine. The Christina River is one of the Delaware River's **tributaries**. It joins Brandywine Creek south of Wilmington. The Chesapeake and Delaware Canal was

WORD TO KNOW

tributaries *smaller rivers that flow into a larger river*

Brandywine Creek in New Castle County

dug across northern Delaware at the narrowest part of the Delmarva Peninsula. This east–west waterway connects the Delaware River with Chesapeake Bay. Many other small rivers, streams, and creeks run through the state. The Nanticoke River of southwestern Delaware continues on through Maryland into Chesapeake Bay.

Along the shores of the Delaware River and Delaware Bay are many inlets and wetlands. Most of the wetlands are saltwater marshes. Some are freshwater marshes, while others are brackish, or a mixture of freshwater and salt water. That's because the freshwater of the Delaware River is mixing with the salty seawater of the Atlantic Ocean.

The shoreline is very different south of Cape Henlopen, where Delaware faces the Atlantic Ocean. This region features sand dunes and long, sandy beaches. Rehoboth Beach, Dewey Beach, and Bethany Beach are popular towns along this coast. Fenwick Island is found along the Delaware and Maryland boundary on the Atlantic Coast.

CLIMATE

Summers in Delaware are sunny and hot. Moisture from the Atlantic Ocean makes the air humid, or moist. At the same time, refreshing ocean breezes keep the coast cooler than the interior. July is the hottest month, with average high temperatures of 86 degrees Fahrenheit (30 degrees Celsius) in New Castle, in the north, and 85°F (29°C) in Lewes, in the south. Heavy thunderstorms often occur in the summer.

Winters are mild. The warm air over the Atlantic Ocean protects much of the state, especially the coastal area, from severe winter weather. Northern Delaware can get colder temperatures than the south. Snowfall is

About 8 percent of Delaware's land area is covered by wetlands.

EXTREME WEATHER

Hurricanes and tropical storms sometimes hit coastal areas. They are dangerous for beachgoers, beachside homes and businesses, and boaters. Delaware has never been hit by the direct landfall of a hurricane. Hurricane Isabel blew through in September 2003. Its high winds and heavy rains flooded rivers and knocked down trees and power lines. This sort of damage is typical of hurricanes that pass by Delaware. Delaware's coast is more often affected by storms known as nor'easters—Atlantic storms with winds from the northeast. These storms move slowly with winds that blow off the ocean and often cause flooding. In 1962, ocean flooding from a nor'easter destroyed many homes along Delaware's Atlantic coast.

Weather Report

This chart shows record temperatures (high and low) for the state, as well as average temperatures (July and January) and average annual precipitation.

Record high temperature	110°F (43°C) at Millsboro on July 21, 1930
Record low temperature	–17°F (–27°C) at Millsboro on January 17, 1893
Average July temperature	77°F (25°C)
Average January temperature	32°F (0°C)
Average yearly precipitation	42 inches (107 cm)

Source: National Climatic Data Center, NESDIS, NOAA, U.S. Dept. of Commerce

heaviest in the north and lightest in the south. January is the coldest month, with an average low temperature of 23°F (–5°C) in New Castle and 26°F (–3°C) in Lewes.

PLANT LIFE

Forests once covered most of Delaware. Today, only about one-third of the state is forested. Common trees in northern Delaware include oak, hickory, beech, maple, sweet gum, and ash. Conifers, or cone-bearing trees, grow in southern Delaware. Red cedars and many pine species flourish in the sandy coastal areas. The American holly, with shiny leaves and red berries, grows here, too. It's the state tree.

Bald cypress trees are common along rivers and in wetlands in the southeastern United States. Although few grow in the north, they are found in Delaware's Trap

Cypress trees growing in Trussum Pond

Pond State Park and Cypress Swamp. These are believed to be the northernmost stands of bald cypresses in the United States.

Delaware farmers grow a variety of flowering fruit trees. The peach blossom became the state flower in 1895. At that time, Delaware led the nation in peach production. Since then, however, disease and harsh weather have severely reduced the peach crop.

Wildflowers brighten the landscape in the spring. Common wildflowers in the state include violets, honeysuckles, crocuses, and asters. The pink lady's slipper, a type of wild orchid, flourishes in swamps and moist forests. Water lilies bloom in the freshwater ponds and lakes, while pink and white hibiscus grow in the saltwater marshes. Bushy plants such as swamp azaleas grow in forested wetlands.

Delaware National Park Areas

This map shows the one site in Delaware protected by the National Park Service.

SEE IT HERE!

BOMBAY HOOK

Bombay Hook National Wildlife Refuge covers about 16,000 acres (6,475 hectares) along the coast northeast of Dover. About four-fifths of that area is tidal salt marshes, areas that fill with salty seawater as the ocean tides rise. The refuge also includes freshwater pools, forests, and grassy fields. Hundreds of thousands of ducks, geese, and shorebirds stop at Bombay Hook on their migrations every year. Tired and hungry, they rest and feast on marsh grasses, fish, and other foods before continuing their flight. Deer, woodchucks, bullfrogs, and **terrapins** also live in the refuge.

WORD TO KNOW

terrapins *turtles that live in fresh or slightly salty water*

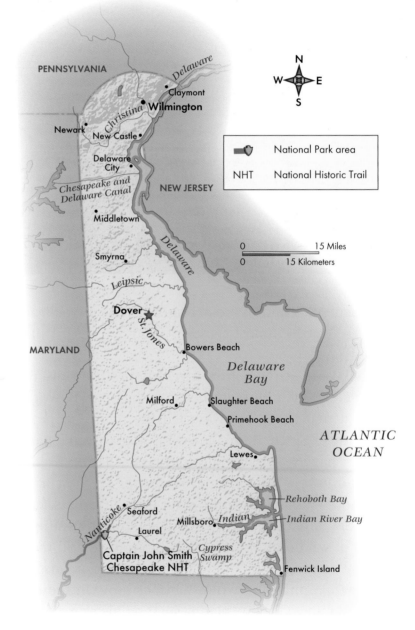

Great egrets at Bombay Hook National Wildlife Refuge

ANIMAL LIFE

White-tailed deer are Delaware's largest wild animals. The state's forests and fields are also home to foxes, rabbits, chipmunks, raccoons, opossums, mink, and moles. Snapping turtles and muskrats live in the marshes and swamps, and diamondback terrapins are found along the coast.

Common Delaware birds include robins, wrens, cardinals, sparrows, orioles, starlings, and warblers. Woodcocks, quails, and pheasants feed on the forest floor. Woodpeckers hammer on tree trunks, and hawks soar overhead. Blue herons, snowy egrets, great egrets, ducks, gulls, and terns search for food along the coast and in marshes. Many of these birds spend their win-

ENDANGERED SEA TURTLES

Several Delaware sea turtle species have been identified as **endangered** or **threatened**. Sea turtles live in the Atlantic Ocean, coming ashore only to nest in the sand. Loggerhead sea turtles are the most common species of sea turtle on Delaware's shores. Loggerheads appear in Delaware Bay in warmer months. They're 31 to 45 inches (79 to 114 centimeters) long, with a reddish-brown to dark-brown, heart-shaped shell. In the summer, young loggerheads swim into Delaware Bay to feed on fish, shellfish, and marine plants. They're often caught in fishing nets by accident. Hawksbill, Kemp's ridley, leatherback, and Atlantic green sea turtles are also endangered or threatened. Human activities and development can endanger these turtles and their nesting grounds.

A young loggerhead turtle

WORDS TO KNOW

endangered *in danger of becoming extinct*

threatened *likely to become an endangered species in the foreseeable future*

ters in Delaware's wetlands. Sandpipers and other species stop by on their seasonal migrations.

Clams and oysters are found in Delaware Bay. The horseshoe crab is an interesting animal common on the coast. Lakes and streams are filled with bass, carp, perch, pike, catfish, and trout. Menhaden, sea trout, shad, and striped bass are some of the fish found in offshore waters.

HUMANS AND THE ENVIRONMENT

Many Delawareans are devoted to protecting their state's natural environment and wildlife. Preserving waters and wetlands is a special priority. The Department of Natural Resources and Environmental Control enforces laws concerning pollution, illegal hunting, and unsafe boating. Citizens' groups such as the Delaware Nature Society also work to preserve Delaware's natural world. They conduct activities such as cleaning up roadways, planting trees, teaching children about the environment, creating wildlife habitats, and monitoring water quality in streams.

The state has protected thousands of acres of land. This includes state parks, forest, and wildlife preserves. Delaware also has passed several environmental laws. One is the Coastal Zone Act of 1971. It protects the Delaware River and Delaware Bay by barring industrial plants being built near the coast where an accident could release harmful chemicals into the waters. Such conservation laws and the efforts of concerned citizens are helping protect Delaware's natural resources for future generations.

Two high school students work in an organic garden in Middletown.

MINI-BIO

RUSSELL PETERSON: DEFENDER OF THE ENVIRONMENT

Long before the environment became a major public issue, Russell Peterson (1916–) was working to protect it. As governor of Delaware (1969–1973), he blocked oil companies from building processing plants along Delaware's coast. He also pushed to pass the Coastal Zone Act, protecting the state's shoreline. Then, as chairman of the Council on Environmental Quality, he worked to ban harmful chemicals used in spray cans. He also served as president of the National Audubon Society. To honor his efforts to protect the environment, the Russell W. Peterson Urban Wildlife Refuge near Wilmington was named in his honor.

? Want to know more? See www.delaware audubon.org/about/board_bios/rpbio.html

READ ABOUT

Native people listen to a storyteller thousands of years ago.

Archaic bannerstones

10,000 BCE

Paleo-Indians live in what is now Delaware

▲ **c. 6500 BCE**

The Archaic culture develops

c. 3000 BCE

People of the early Woodland period begin gathering shellfish and making pottery

CHAPTER TWO

FIRST PEOPLE

★

S OME 20,000 YEARS AGO, AN ICE AGE GRIPPED THE PLANET. With so much water frozen into ice, sea levels were much lower than they are today. A strip of land between what are now Alaska and Russia rose above the surface of the water. People from Asia walked across this land to North America. Over the centuries, they spread across the continent, reaching today's Delaware at least 12,000 years ago.

c. 1000 CE
People of the late
Woodland period begin
hunting with bows
and arrows

1400s ▶
Lenapes live in the
Delaware River valley

Lenape pot

1600s
The lives of Nanticokes
and Lenapes are changed
by European explorers

These remains were discovered at Island Field Site, a Native American burial ground near Bowers Beach.

WORDS TO KNOW

nomadic *describing someone who moves from place to place and does not permanently settle in one location*

archaeologists *people who study the remains of past human societies*

PALEO-INDIANS AND ARCHAIC PEOPLES

Delaware's earliest residents were **nomadic** hunters and gatherers. Called Paleo-Indians, they lived in the region by 10,000 BCE. The climate was colder than it is now, and spruce forests covered much of the landscape. The Paleo-Indians gathered wild plants and hunted deer and other forest animals, using spears with sharp, stone-pointed tips. They made other stone tools to scrape the hides and cut up meat. **Archaeologists** believe the Paleo-Indians lived and traveled in small family groups. They took advantage of good hunting grounds in what is now southern Delaware and then moved north to obtain the hard stone they needed for making tools.

Around 6500 BCE, Delaware's Native people entered a new period, called the Archaic. The climate had become warmer and wetter, and water gathered in many pools and ponds across the landscape. Animals came to drink at these watering holes, and Archaic people hunted them. Edible plants were abundant, too. People gathered seeds, nuts, and other plant foods and used stone tools to grind them up.

Native American Peoples

(Before European Contact)

This map shows the general area of Native American peoples before
European settlers arrived.

A Woodland hunter brings food home to his family.

WOODLAND CULTURES

Delaware's Woodland cultures began to emerge around 3000 BCE. Around this time, the climate became warmer and drier. Large marshes appeared along the coast, and rivers flowed through the interior. In this new environment, people adapted to new ways of life.

Archaeologists divide the Woodland era into an early period and a late period. In the early period, people lived near the marshes and along the rivers. Much of their diet consisted of shellfish—especially oysters—and fish. Sometimes they ventured into the forests to hunt and gather plants. In riverside camps, people lived in wigwams. These were large, dome-shaped houses with wood frames and bark coverings. Some wigwams had indoor fireplaces and deep pits for storing food. People also began making clay pottery at this time. They lived in small family groups that were isolated from one another, rather than in villages.

The late Woodland period began around 1000 CE. During this time, Delaware's Woodland people began carving designs into their pottery, and men began hunting with bows and arrows. In other parts of the mid-Atlantic region, people were settling in villages and cultivating corn, beans, and squash. This may have been happening in Delaware, too, but scientists have not yet found evidence of this way of life there.

THE LENAPE PEOPLE

By the 1400s, the Lenape people were living in the Delaware River valley. The Lenape homeland stretched from today's Delaware into New Jersey, Pennsylvania, and New York. Northern and central Delaware marked their southernmost territory. The Lenape people are also called Lenni Lenapes, meaning "true people" or "original people." Europeans called them Delawares, after the river.

Lenapes spoke a language that belonged to the Algonquian language family. Algonquian speakers once ranged across the northern Atlantic coast, the Great Lakes region, parts of the Midwest, and much of Canada. The Lenape are considered the most ancient of all the Algonquian peoples. Other Algonquian-speaking peoples traditionally honored them as ancestors. Lenapes were also respected as peacemakers, and other Algonquian groups often sought their help in resolving disputes.

The Lenape people had no central leader. Rather, they were organized into clans, each of which was made up of related families. Those who lived in what is now

Woodland arrow

Lenape clay pot

Delaware belonged to the clans called Unami, meaning "people downriver," and Unalachtigo, meaning "people who live near the ocean." Membership in a clan was passed down through the mother. That is, children in each family belonged to their mother's clan.

Farther north, Lenapes lived in longhouses that were sometimes 150 feet (46 m) long and housed several families. But Delaware's Lenape people lived in single-family wigwams, as their Woodland ancestors had. Men cut small trees for the wigwam frames, and women built the dwellings, covering them with bark or woven mats. Extended family groups banded together in small, independent villages. The oldest woman in each group appointed a sachem, or chief. The sachem and other community leaders formed a council to make decisions for the village.

Lenapes carried on extensive farming. In the spring, men cleared the fields and broke up the soil so it was ready for planting. Women sowed beans, squash, and corn and tended the crops. Women also gathered wild plants, cooked, made clothing from animal hides, and took care of the children. Lenape men made tools, hunted deer and other wild animals with bows and arrows, and caught fish in nets of woven branches or grasses. In the winter, small

Picture Yourself . . .

Building a Lenape Wigwam

Your family has just moved to a new riverside camp, so you join in to help build a wigwam for shelter. Your father heads into the forest to chop down some fine saplings, or young trees, for the frame. Meanwhile, down by the river, you and your mother gather armloads of tall grasses. Then you sit down and weave them tightly into flat mats. It's summertime, and the mats will make a fine covering for the wigwam.

When your father returns with the saplings, you use a sharp stone to remove any leaves and small branches. You drive one end of each sapling deep into the soil, placing them in a circular pattern. You help your mother bend the top ends around and drive them in the ground, too. Now you have the dome-shaped frame. You curve branches around the sides for support, lashing them in place with tough plant fibers. Finally, you lay the mats on the frame, tying each one to secure it. You leave a hole in the top of the wigwam for smoke from the cooking fire to escape. Finally, you go inside and lay mats on the floor for sleeping. At last, your new home is ready!

This village shows a Lenape wigwam (left) and longhouse.

family groups traveled around hunting together. On trips to the coast, they gathered shellfish such as oysters and clams. Children learned adult responsibilities by helping out with their parents' chores.

Each village had sweat lodges where villagers took steam baths. People heated stones in the lodge and poured water over them to create steam. Sweating in the steam was believed to relieve ailments and purify the spirit.

For recreation, Lenapes played a number of games. One was a type of football game called *pahsaheman*. The ball was made of deerskin stuffed with deer hair. Women were on one side, and men were on the other. The men could only kick the ball, but the women could throw it or pick it up and run.

SEE IT HERE!

NANTICOKE INDIAN MUSEUM

The Nanticoke Indian Museum in Millsboro is housed in a building that used to be a one-room schoolhouse. The museum gives you a glimpse into the traditional Nanticoke way of life. It displays intricately beaded jewelry, as well as clothing, pottery, and pine-needle baskets used by the Nanticokes' ancestors. Spears, arrowheads, hammers, and various other tools show how the Nanticokes relied on hunting, fishing, and farming. Some items date back as early as 10,000 BCE. The museum also contains a library of materials related to Native Americans.

THE NANTICOKE PEOPLE

Another Native American group, the Nanticoke people, made their home in today's southern Delaware and Maryland. Their territory extended across the Delmarva Peninsula from Delaware Bay to Chesapeake Bay. The Nanticokes' name means "tidewater people." Like Lenapes, Nanticokes are Algonquian speakers. They originated among the Lenape people and share their ancient heritage.

Nanticoke homes were wigwams with a curved shape, like Lenape shelters. Nanticokes occupied permanent summer villages, where they survived by hunting, fishing, trapping, and farming. Men made nets, baskets, and spears to catch fish and eels. They also gathered clams, oysters, mussels, and crabs. Using bows and arrows, they hunted squirrels, turkeys, deer, rabbits, ducks, and geese. In the winter, families left their villages on hunting expeditions.

Farming was possible in areas where the ground was not marshy. Men cleared trees from a patch of forest, and women loosened the soil using branches or hoes made of shell, bone, or stone. They planted corn, beans, squash, pumpkins, sunflowers, and tobacco. Children helped out by weeding the gardens and scaring away birds. Children also helped their mothers gather birds' eggs, as well as nuts, berries, and other edible plants.

Both men and women wore an apronlike garment, leggings, robes, and moccasins. Women made these clothes out of deerskin. First, they scraped the

Nanticokes made baskets like this one from grass. It is decorated with a clamshell.

fur and fat off the skin and softened it. Then, using a bone needle, they sewed beads or shells on the clothing for decorations. In the winter, people wore cloaks of deerskin or bearskin with the fur on the inside.

Women cut up the animals and prepared meals. They ground corn into meal. To make a kind of bread called pone, they mixed the cornmeal with water and baked it on a hot stone. Fish were cooked on wood racks over a fire or on sticks stuck into the ground around the fire. Women stored extra food in underground pits or in baskets they wove of grasses or bark.

The Nanticoke people carried on extensive trade with groups in the Ohio River valley, to the northwest. Nanticoke traders provided sharks' teeth and beads made of oyster and clamshells. In exchange, they received clay pipes, copper beads, and knives.

But change was on the horizon. In the 1600s, people from distant lands would sail into Delaware Bay, changing the lives of the Nanticoke and Lenape peoples forever.

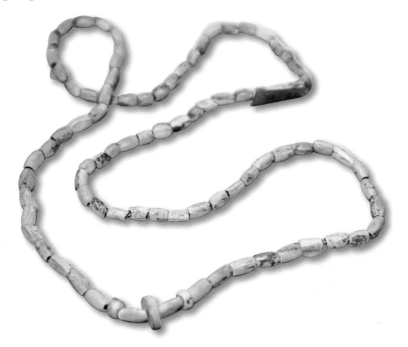

A string of shell beads used as money by the Nanticoke people

READ ABOUT

Swedish settlers at Paradise Point, 1600s

1609 ►

Henry Hudson sails into Delaware Bay

1638

Swedish colonists establish Fort Christina, Delaware's first permanent European settlement

1682

Englishman William Penn gains control of Delaware

William Penn addressing Swedish colonists, late 1600s

in England. He wanted his colony to be a place where his fellow Quakers, and people of all faiths, could enjoy religious freedom. Pennsylvania had no land facing the Atlantic Ocean, so in 1682, Penn obtained the land that is now Delaware from the Duke of York. The three counties making up that land—New Castle, Kent, and Sussex, from north to south—became known as Pennsylvania's Three Lower Counties. Penn first set foot in his new colony when he sailed into New Castle in 1682.

People from many different backgrounds settled in Delaware. The promise of religious freedom was a big attraction. There were English Quakers and Anglicans, Scots-Irish Presbyterians, Swedish and German Lutherans, and Dutch people who belonged to the Dutch Reformed Church. Other settlers had come from Finland, France, and nearby colonies.

Pennsylvania's colonial government ruled the Three Lower Counties. People in the Lower Counties didn't like being ruled by Pennsylvania, however. They

thought they didn't have much of a voice in their own government. In 1701, representatives of the Three Lower Counties asked Penn's permission to form their own legislature, or lawmaking assembly. Penn agreed. Delaware's legislature met for the first time in 1704. Governors of the Pennsylvania Colony still ruled the three counties, though.

Most people in the Three Lower Counties were farmers. They shipped grain and dairy products to England and other countries. For people who lived along the coast, fishing was an important occupation. Some people operated mills along Brandywine Creek. As the water rushed by, it turned huge mill wheels that powered small factories such as flour mills and leather tanneries. Quakers founded Wilmington in 1739. It became known for shipbuilding.

In southern Delaware, farming was the main occupation. Many of the farmers were English people who had come from Maryland and other neighboring colonies. They brought Africans to work as slaves on their farms. Africans cleared the land and grew wheat, corn, and tobacco. Then they harvested the crops and prepared them for shipping. By 1763, one-quarter of the residents of Delaware were of African descent, and their labor was crucial to the colony's survival.

THE FATE OF NATIVE AMERICANS

By this time, few Native Americans remained in Delaware. European settlers had crowded them out of their land. Europeans made one land treaty after another with the Lenape people, but the treaties were disasters. The European settlers routinely broke the agreements, and the Lenape people did not understand the European concept of land ownership. Lenapes

William Penn (eighth from the right with arms outstretched) in a treaty discussion with Native Americans

believed they were granting Europeans the right to *share* Lenape land, not take it over.

Delaware's Lenape people were eventually pushed north into New Jersey and New York, and west into Pennsylvania, Ohio, and beyond. Because of settlers' wars and diseases, Lenape numbers were reduced from an estimated 20,000 people in 1600 to 4,000 in 1700.

The Nanticoke people suffered a similar fate. By 1750, settlers had crowded them out of their last villages on the Delmarva Peninsula. Some Nanticokes moved east, settling in southern New Jersey and in the Indian River area on Delaware's coast. Others moved into Pennsylvania and New York, where they allied themselves with the Iroquois. They and other groups formed a union of six Native American nations, which was centered in northern New York. Other Nanticokes joined with Lenape groups and moved west. Still others stayed behind, merged into white society, and lost their traditions.

DELAWARE'S MOORS

People traditionally called Moors were living in Kent and Sussex counties by the 1700s. Their ancestry is believed to be a mixture of Nanticoke, European, and possibly African. Several legends exist about them, but their exact origins are unknown. The Moors, most of whom lived near Cheswold and Millsboro, maintained separate communities, identifying with none of their ancestral groups. Descendants of the Moors still exist today, though few remain in their original communities.

WAR AND INDEPENDENCE

Eventually, 13 colonies grew up along the Atlantic Coast. By this time, England had formed a political union with Scotland and was called Great Britain. American colonists paid taxes to Great Britain, which they resented because they had no voice in their government. "No taxation without representation!" became their slogan. Many colonists wanted to pull away and form an independent nation. This conflict led to the Revolutionary War (1775–1783). John Dickinson of Kent County argued passionately for independence. His essays in favor of revolution inspired people throughout the colonies to seek independence.

A group of delegates signing the Declaration of Independence, 1776

In 1776, American colonists announced their freedom from Great Britain in the Declaration of Independence. This document declared that the colonies were now the United States of America. Among those who signed the declaration were Thomas McKean, George Read, and Caesar Rodney of Delaware. In June 1776, Delaware also declared its freedom from Pennsylvania. The Three Lower Counties now called themselves the state of Delaware. They drew up their first state constitution, or basic set of laws, and made New Castle their capital.

Almost 4,000 Delawareans signed up to fight in the Revolutionary War. The only battle on Delaware soil was the Battle of Cooch's Bridge, which took place near Newark, in the northern part of the colony, on September 3, 1777. The colonists lost this battle, but they won the war.

Delaware's economy grew quickly after the war. By this time, the Wilmington area led the nation in flour milling—grinding grains such as wheat, rye, corn, and oats into flour.

MINI-BIO

JOHN DICKINSON: PENMAN OF THE REVOLUTION

In the 1760s, John Dickinson (1732–1808) wrote a series of essays in favor of independence. They were so powerful that he came to be called the Penman of the Revolution. He served as president (governor) of both Pennsylvania and Delaware. He was also Delaware's wealthiest farmer. Poplar Hall, his home in Kent County, was the center of a large plantation that employed enslaved Africans. Dickinson was a devout Quaker, and many Quakers disapproved of slavery. In 1777, he freed all his slaves.

? Want to know more? See www.state.de.us/facts/history/dicknbio.htm

CAESAR RODNEY'S HEROIC RIDE

Caesar Rodney was one of Delaware's three representatives to the Continental Congress, the group of leaders who led the colonies before and during the American Revolution. The Continental Congress met in Philadelphia, Pennsylvania. In June 1776, members of the Continental Congress discussed independence from Great Britain. Following these discussions, Rodney returned home to Dover.

On July 1, Congress decided to vote on independence. Each colony would get only one vote, based on the vote of its representatives in Congress. Delaware's other two representatives were split, with one for and one against independence. When Rodney heard this, he jumped on his horse—even though he was seriously ill—and rode through a thunderstorm on the night of July 1–2, arriving just in time to cast his vote for independence. An image of Rodney on horseback appears on Delaware's state quarter.

This process required backbreaking labor. In 1785, Oliver Evans of Newport invented a machine that milled flour automatically. This transformed the flour-milling industry, making the process easier and faster than ever before.

BECOMING THE FIRST STATE

In 1787, representatives of all the states met at the Constitutional Convention in Philadelphia. Their aim was to draw up the U.S. Constitution. As soon as each state ratified, or approved, the Constitution, it would become an official U.S. state. John Dickinson and George Read were two of Delaware's representatives at the convention, and they helped write the document.

Some representatives at the convention wanted to create a two-house Congress, with all its members elected according to population. That would give states with large populations much more power than states with small populations. Read insisted that small states such as Delaware should have the same say as large states. Finally, a compromise was reached. Members of the House of Representatives would be elected according to population, but all states would be represented equally in the Senate.

With this compromise, Read urged his fellow Delawareans to approve the Constitution. On December 7, 1787, Delaware was the first state to ratify the U.S. Constitution. In doing so, it became the first official state of the new United States. That is why Delaware proudly calls itself the First State.

After the Revolutionary War, about 130 flour mills were active in the Wilmington area. They produced tens of thousands of barrels of flour every year.

The U.S. Constitution

Delaware: From Colony to Statehood
(1704–1787)

This map shows the Delaware colony that later became the state of Delaware in 1787.

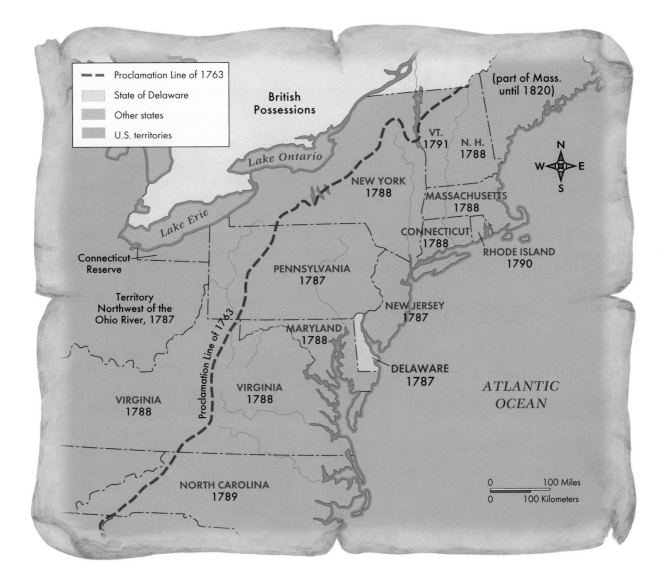

Proclamation Line of 1763
State of Delaware
Other states
U.S. territories

British Possessions

(part of Mass. until 1820)

VT. 1791

N. H. 1788

Lake Ontario

NEW YORK 1788

MASSACHUSETTS 1788

CONNECTICUT 1788

RHODE ISLAND 1790

Lake Erie

Connecticut Reserve

PENNSYLVANIA 1787

Territory Northwest of the Ohio River, 1787

Proclamation Line of 1763

NEW JERSEY 1787

MARYLAND 1788

DELAWARE 1787

VIRGINIA 1788

VIRGINIA 1788

ATLANTIC OCEAN

NORTH CAROLINA 1789

N
W E
S

0   100 Miles
0   100 Kilometers

44

Mills on
Brandywine
Creek, 1800s

1802

*Éleuthère Irénée du
Pont de Nemours opens
a gunpowder mill on
Brandywine Creek*

▲**1813**

*Peter Spencer forms
the African Union
Church*

1829

*The Chesapeake
and Delaware Canal
opens, connecting
Delaware Bay and
Chesapeake Bay*

CHAPTER FOUR

GROWTH AND CHANGE

★

IN THE EARLY 1800s, FARMING WAS STILL DELAWARE'S KEY ECONOMIC ACTIVITY. But new industries were springing up. Mills were opening near Wilmington, along the swift-flowing Brandy-wine Creek. One was Gilpin's Mill, the nation's first paper mill. Other mills turned out flour, cotton cloth, leather, and lumber.

1847
An act to abolish slavery narrowly fails in the Delaware Senate

1861–65 ►
Delaware remains in the Union during the Civil War

DELAWARE

1920
For the first time, more Delawareans live in urban areas than in rural areas

This gunpowder mill on Brandywine Creek was opened by Éleuthère Irénée du Pont de Nemours in 1802.

THE DU PONTS ARRIVE

A French immigrant named Éleuthère Irénée du Pont de Nemours had a tremendous impact on Delaware. In 1802, he opened a gunpowder mill on Brandywine Creek near Greenville. By 1820, it was the leading supplier of gunpowder for the U.S. government. This mill would later grow into the DuPont Company, one of the largest chemical companies in the world. Members of the du Pont family would be prominent figures in Delaware business, politics, and culture for more than two centuries.

Delaware was becoming a crossroads for water and railroad transportation. Goods shipped between Philadelphia and Baltimore, Maryland, often had to pass through Delaware. Many Delaware products were destined for markets in those cities, too. In 1828, steamboats began running between New Castle and Philadelphia. The Chesapeake and Delaware Canal opened in 1829. Cutting through northern Delaware, it provided a water route between Delaware Bay and Maryland's Chesapeake Bay. The New Castle and Frenchtown Railroad began operating in 1832, and the Philadelphia, Wilmington and Baltimore Railroad opened in 1838.

SLAVERY AND ABOLITION

Before the American Revolution, slavery was allowed throughout the colonies. But by 1804, all northern states had passed laws that would eventually end slavery. In the South, however, where enslaved workers were used as labor on large-scale farms, slavery was widespread. Delaware lay on the border between the North and the South. It allowed slavery, but there were Delawareans on both sides of the issue.

During the Revolutionary War, antislavery societies, often led by Quakers, had sprouted in Delaware and other states. The members of such societies believed that slavery could not exist in a country devoted to freedom.

In 1847, the Delaware Senate voted on a bill to abolish slavery. It was defeated by just one vote. By this time, many Delawareans, especially Quakers, were fierce **abolitionists**. The Quaker John Dickinson, once Delaware's largest slaveholder, had freed all his slaves in 1777. Others followed his example. By 1860, the state's largest slaveholder had just 16 slaves.

SEE IT HERE!

GREENBANK MILL

Greenbank Mill in Wilmington has been a flour mill, a wool textile factory, and a woodworking plant. Built in the 1760s, it was devastated by a fire in 1969. It has since been restored and now offers visitors a realistic glimpse into life in a mill town between 1790 and 1830. Join a weekend tour, and you'll take part in millworkers' daily chores and try your hand at their trades.

WORD TO KNOW

abolitionists *people who work to end slavery*

A group of enslaved people flees the Maryland coast to an Underground Railroad depot in Delaware in 1850.

Q8 WHY WERE QUAKERS SO ACTIVE IN THE ABOLITIONIST MOVEMENT?

A8 Quakers believe that the same divine light burns within all people. Therefore, everyone is equal in the eyes of God. Beginning in the 1700s, Quakers were the first white people in Great Britain and its colonies to fight against slavery and the slave trade. Quakers also supported equal rights for women and opposed war.

Free African Americans made up a large share of Delaware's population. Of the 90,000 people living in Delaware in 1860, almost 20,000 were free African Americans. Some had come from other states, and some were native Delawareans. Some had once been enslaved, while others had been free all their lives. By this time, fewer than one in ten African Americans in Delaware was enslaved.

In Delaware, free people of color had few rights. They could not vote, serve on a jury, testify against a white person, or serve in the militia. The black community knew it had to aid its members, and they established many of their own churches and schools.

THE UNDERGROUND RAILROAD

Delawareans played a major role in the Underground Railroad, a secret network of people who helped those fleeing slavery escape to freedom in the North. In the dark of night, the **fugitives** crossed marshes, forests, and rivers. They risked drowning, faced snakes and wild animals, and suffered hunger and exhaustion. People opposed to slavery, both black and white, helped them on their way.

All along the escape routes, people provided boats, carriages, and hiding places in their homes, churches, and barns. John Hunn, a Kent County Quaker, kept up his Underground Railroad activities even after being convicted and fined for helping runaway slaves. Thomas Garrett, a Quaker merchant in Wilmington, sheltered thousands of people freeing slavery. He worked closely with Harriet Tubman. After escaping slavery herself, Tubman helped hundreds of others escape to the North.

Garrett also worked with Samuel Burris, a free African American, and they both suffered for their courage. Garrett was arrested and fined so many times, he said to a judge: "Thee hasn't left me a dollar, but I wish to say to thee, and to all in the courtroom, that if anyone knows a fugitive who wants shelter, and a friend, send him to Thomas Garrett, and he will befriend him." Burris was arrested for aiding fugitives

MINI-BIO

PETER SPENCER: FOUNDER OF THE AFRICAN UNION CHURCH

Born into slavery in Maryland, Peter Spencer (c. 1779—1843) was freed when his owner died. Then he moved to Wilmington. He was fervently religious and taught fellow African Americans to read and write, believing the combination of education and religion gave his people power. In 1813, he founded the African Union Church, the country's first independent black church. He also established the Big August Quarterly, an annual gathering of church members that is still celebrated in Wilmington today.

? Want to know more? See www.motherafricanunion.org/about_us

Before the Civil War, Delaware had the country's largest population of free African Americans.

WORD TO KNOW

fugitives *people who flee or escape*

THOMAS GARRETT: ABOLITIONIST

Thomas Garrett (1789–1871) was a devout Quaker and an ardent abolitionist. He helped as many as 2,700 fugitive slaves reach freedom on the Underground Railroad. Garrett and his wife hid runaway slaves in their home in Wilmington. This was the fugitives' last stop on the way to freedom in Pennsylvania. Before sneaking them across the border, Garrett gave them food, shoes, and clothing for their journey. He was one of the busiest "station masters" on the Underground Railroad.

❓ **Want to know more?** See www.hsd.org/ DHE/DHE_who_garrett.htm

A memorial to the Delaware soldiers who fought at the Battle of Gettysburg (Pennsylvania) during the Civil War

and punished by being auctioned off as a slave. Garrett saved him by sending friends to buy him. They then freed him again. Burris left for California as a free man.

THE CIVIL WAR

The conflict surrounding slavery and states' rights led to the Civil War (1861–1865). Eleven Southern states pulled away from the Union and formed the Confederate States of America. Northern states fought to preserve the Union. Delaware remained in the Union, although

DELAWARE

many Delawareans sympathized with the Confederacy.

During the war, many enslaved Delawareans fled bondage and, like many free black Delawareans, joined the Union forces. They were among the more than 200,000 African Americans who helped to ensure a Union victory in 1865. After this, all enslaved people in Delaware and the United States were freed.

NEW OPPORTUNITIES AND SEGREGATION

After the Civil War, Delaware's African American community continued to grow. In cities and rural areas alike, African Americans worked as both professionals and skilled tradesmen. Their occupations included shopkeepers, barbers, tailors, blacksmiths, cabinetmakers, shipbuilders, fishers, and farmers.

State laws, however, prevented African Americans in Delaware from enjoying their full rights as citizens. A state **poll tax** kept many black citizens from voting. They had to maintain separate housing from whites and were not allowed in whites-only hotels and restaurants. Despite all these restrictions, in 1901, Thomas Postles won election as the first African American on the Wilmington city council.

In Delaware, many African Americans struggled to receive an education. From 1866 to 1876, the Delaware

MINI-BIO

MARY ANN SHADD CARY: ABOLITIONIST AND LAWYER

Mary Ann Shadd Cary (1823–1893) was born in Wilmington, the oldest of 13 children. Her parents were free African Americans, and their home was a stop on the Underground Railroad. In 1851, she moved to Canada. There she became the first African American woman in North America to edit a newspaper—the antislavery Provincial Freeman. Cary later returned to the United States and became the nation's second black woman to earn a law degree. She went on to fight for women's right to vote.

? **Want to know more?** See www.nps.gov/nr/travel/underground/dc2.htm

WORD TO KNOW

poll tax *a fee a person must pay before he or she can vote*

One of Delaware's segregated schools, 1922

Association for the Moral Improvement and Education of Colored People—whose members were both black and white—built 32 elementary schools for African American children in the state. In 1875, Delaware began funding public schools for African American children, but until 1881, those funds had to come from black taxpayers.

Then in 1896, the U.S. Supreme Court ruled in *Plessy v. Ferguson* that it was lawful to provide "separate but equal" schools for African American and white children. In reality, however, there was nothing equal about the **segregated** schools. Between 1910 and 1920, white schools received 10 times more funding than black schools.

FARMS AND FACTORIES

Delaware's farms and factories flourished after the war. Farmers were able to ship their products to market on newly built railroads. This encouraged more farming in southern Delaware. Peaches were a booming crop, reaching their record year in 1875. Farmers were raising tons of peas, tomatoes, and other crops, too.

Many fruit and vegetable **canneries** opened in Kent and Sussex counties. In 1880, 15 percent of the workers in Delaware's fruit and vegetable canneries were children. Boys and girls as young as five years old hauled buckets of peaches, peas, and other crops. They sorted and helped can them. The children labored 10, 12, or even more hours a day, working near moving machine parts and boiling-hot cans.

WORD TO KNOW

canneries *factories where food is canned*

An eight-year-old girl (center) works with other children at a cannery in Seaford in 1910.

LICE PAUL
OT SEVEN MONTHS
BECAUSE
OPPOSED A POLITICAL PARTY
WE DEMAND
T SHE BE TREATED AS A
POLITICAL OFFENDER

THE SUFFRAGE PRISONERS
WERE ARRESTED FOR A
POLITICAL OFFENSE.
WE DEMAND
THAT THEY BE TREATED AS
POLITICAL OFFENDERS.

TO ASK FREEDOM
FOR WOMEN IS NOT
A CRIME
SUFFRAGE PRISONER
SHOULD NOT BE TREATED
AS CRIMINALS

THE STRUGGLE FOR THE VOTE

In the early 20th century, many women in Delaware began fighting for their right to vote. They held meetings, gave speeches, and tried to convince lawmakers to change the state constitution. But in 1913 and 1915, the Delaware General Assembly rejected laws that would allow women to vote. Delaware women then began holding parades and protests in support of their right to vote. In 1917, several women from Delaware traveled to Washington, D.C., to protest outside the White House, demanding that President Woodrow Wilson take action. Some of these women, including Mabel Vernon and Florence Bayard Hilles, were arrested.

Eventually, Wilson began to support their cause, and in 1919, Congress passed an amendment, or change, to the U.S. Constitution, giving women the right to vote. By August 1920, enough states had ratified the amendment for it to go into effect. Finally, women had the same voting rights as men.

These women from Delaware and other states marched in 1917 to protest the imprisonment of a suffrage leader.

At the same time, industries in the Wilmington area were also growing quickly. Thousands of immigrants came to work in the city's shipyards, iron foundries, machine shops, and factories. They came from Ireland, Germany, Poland, Italy, Russia, and many other countries.

By the time of World War I (1914–1918), the DuPont Company was the nation's largest producer of gunpowder. It supplied tons of explosives for the U.S. armed forces. Iron making, shipbuilding, and many other industries helped the war effort, too. All these activities created more jobs, and people from outlying areas moved into Wilmington and other cities to work. By 1920, more Delawareans lived in urban areas than in rural areas. Delaware was well on its way to becoming an industrial state.

A view of Tenth Street in Wilmington, early 1900s

MINI-BIO

ANNIE JUMP CANNON: STARSTRUCK

As a child in Dover, Annie Jump Cannon (1863–1941) loved star-gazing. When she went to Wellesley College in Massachusetts, she became one of the first women from Delaware to attend college. She studied physics and astronomy and graduated in 1884. She returned to Delaware for 10 years but couldn't resist the lure of astronomy. In the 1890s, she began working at the Harvard College Observatory in Massachusetts. There she measured and listed more than 200,000 stars and discovered 300 new ones. The system she developed for classifying stars is still used today.

? Want to know more? See www.hsd.org/DHE/DHE_who_jump-cannon.htm

Lockerman Street in Dover, 1920s

1924
The DuPont Highway, the first highway to run through Delaware from north to south, opens

▲**1929**
Louis Redding becomes the state's first African American lawyer

1950
The University of Delaware begins admitting African American students

CHAPTER FIVE

MORE MODERN TIMES

★

IN THE 1920s, DELAWARE'S FACTORIES WERE HUMMING. More people were buying automobiles, and they were enjoying new inventions such as motion pictures and radios. But trouble was on the horizon. In the 1930s, the Great Depression swept the nation. This economic disaster brought about widespread unemployment and bank collapses. The Depression did not hit Delaware as hard as it hit many other states. Still, thousands of Delawareans lost their jobs.

1971

The Delaware Coastal Zone Act bans industrial plants along the state's coastline

1981

The Financial Center Development Act encourages banks to locate in Delaware

2000 ▶

Ruth Ann Minner is elected Delaware's first female governor

A WPA mural being painted in Wilmington, 1930s

DEPRESSION AND WAR

In 1933, President Franklin D. Roosevelt took office. He started a series of programs called the New Deal to put people back to work and get the country moving again. One program, the Farm Security Administration (FSA), paid photographers to document Delaware's farm life. Through the Works Progress Administration (WPA), writers were paid to write books on the state of Delaware and the city of Newport. The WPA also paid artists to create murals and other paintings in the state. The Civilian Conservation Corps (CCC) employed young men to work on outdoor construction projects. In Delaware, there were CCC camps in Lewes, Leipsic, and several other towns. Workers lived in the camps while they planted trees and built roads and park facilities. CCC workers also dug ditches across coastal marshes to drain the water. This was intended to control mosquitoes, which lay their eggs in wetlands.

The DuPont Company stayed active throughout the Depression. It developed a new fiber called nylon in the 1930s. In 1939, DuPont opened the world's first nylon plant in Seaford. Nylon is an artificial substitute for expensive silk, and women's nylon stockings would turn out to be a popular product.

During World War II (1939–1945), about 30,000 Delawareans—men and women of all races—signed up to serve in the armed forces. The U.S. government built military air bases at New Castle and Dover. It also built Fort Miles on Cape Henlopen. Delaware's farms, factories, and mills went into high gear to produce supplies for the troops. They turned out canned foods, ships, airplanes, iron, steel, and other goods. DuPont's nylon was also helpful. It was used for military supplies such as parachutes, tents, and bomber tires.

POSTWAR GROWTH

After the war, Delaware welcomed new industries and saw old industries expand. Large corporations such as General Motors and General Foods opened plants in the state. The DuPont Company opened more research centers to develop new chemical products. It became the state's largest private employer until the 1980s.

In Sussex County, the chicken industry expanded and more resorts grew up along the shore. Dover Air Force Base brought many new jobs to the Dover area. The

DU PONTS IN THE 1920s

The du Pont family made many contributions to Delaware in the 1920s. Pierre S. du Pont (shown here) was the great-grandson of the DuPont Company's founder. He donated several million dollars to build new public schools, mostly for African American students. He also gave a great deal of money to the University of Delaware. His cousin T. Coleman du Pont built the first highway to run through Delaware from north to south. Called the DuPont Highway, it opened in 1924. Another cousin, Alfred I. du Pont, built Delaware's first welfare home. All three held public offices in the state, in addition to managing the family business.

In its first year of operation, DuPont's factory in Seaford produced enough nylon to make 64 million pairs of stockings!

SEE IT HERE!

SEAFORD MUSEUM

At the Seaford Museum in the city of Seaford, you can explore hundreds of years of regional history. You'll see a nylon-spinning machine from DuPont's 1939 nylon factory. You'll also learn about the region's canning, shipbuilding, and chicken industries. Other exhibits feature Nanticoke life and culture, Revolutionary War soldiers, and outlaws. There is also a display about Governor William Ross, a Seaford resident in the 1800s. Visitors can tour the nearby Ross mansion and see its horse stables, smokehouse, and slave quarters.

Delaware Memorial Bridge, which spans the Delaware River, opened in 1951. For the first time, people could drive directly between Delaware and New Jersey. In Wilmington and Dover, suburbs began to expand far beyond the city limits.

THE CIVIL RIGHTS MOVEMENT

Delaware had been a leader in the antislavery movement of the 1800s. At a time when slavery was an accepted institution, Delaware had a record number of free African Americans. But a century later, citizenship, freedom, and equality were still far away for people of color in the state.

Delaware still had laws that separated blacks from white Delawareans in workplaces, schools, restaurants, and movie theaters. Employers could refuse to hire African Americans and almost always paid them lower wages. In Wilmington, most African Americans were poor and lived in segregated neighborhoods.

An aerial view of the Delaware Memorial Bridge, which opened in 1951

These white students return to school in Milford following a 1954 protest of the admission of African American students.

MINI-BIO

LOUIS REDDING: LAWYER AND ACTIVIST

Louis Redding (1901–1998) grew up in one of Wilmington's segregated neighborhoods. He attended Howard High School, the only high school for blacks in Delaware at the time. In 1929, he became Delaware's first African American attorney, and he soon began working to protect the **civil rights** of all Delawareans. Redding used his talents as a lawyer to end segregation at the University of Delaware and other schools. He was also part of the legal team that presented the Brown v. Board of Education case to the U.S. Supreme Court.

? **Want to know more?** See http://query.nytimes.com/gst/fullpage.html?res=9F06E7D61538F931A35753C1A96E958260

Blacks increasingly began to challenge racial segregation. In 1947, William J. Winchester became the first African American elected to the Delaware state legislature. Delaware lawyer Louis Redding worked hard for equality in education. His efforts led a Delaware court to order the University of Delaware to admit black students in 1950. Redding filed more lawsuits in the 1950s charging that "separate but equal" schools for black and white children went against the U.S. Constitution. In 1952, a Delaware judge ruled in his favor, and in 1954, the U.S. Supreme Court agreed in the *Brown v. Board of Education* decision.

WORD TO KNOW

civil rights *basic human rights that all citizens in a society are entitled to, such as the right to vote*

Members of the Ku Klux Klan hold a rally in Delaware in 1967.

discrimination *unequal treatment based on race, gender, religion, or other factors*

In 1963, Delaware outlawed racial segregation in public places such as restaurants. The Ku Klux Klan tried to frighten African Americans by using violence and acts of terrorism. When civil rights leader Martin Luther King Jr. was assassinated in 1968, riots broke out in Wilmington and across the country. The governor called out the National Guard to keep order. The National Guard remained in Wilmington for nine months. That same year, Delaware passed a law ending racial **discrimination** in housing throughout the state.

But segregation continued in many public schools because black and white Delawareans lived in separate neighborhoods. In 1978, the Wilmington area was required to send children to schools outside their neighborhoods so that the schools would be more ethnically and economically diverse. This was discontinued in 1995.

THE ENVIRONMENT AND NEW BUSINESSES

In the 1960s, many people began to be concerned about preserving the environment. In 1971, the Delaware legislature passed the Coastal Zone Act, which barred companies from building industrial plants along the state's coast. In 2002, Delaware passed the Clean Indoor Air Act, which banned smoking in public places.

Throughout the 1970s, economic development in northern Delaware was slowing down. To help revive the region's economy, in 1981, the state passed the Financial Center Development Act. It

WOMEN'S RIGHTS ACTIVIST

Helen Thomas (1921–) is an activist for women's rights. Women had gained the right to vote in 1920. But Thomas believed that women still had a long way to go to achieve equality. A wife, mother of three, and college English teacher, she helped organize Delaware's chapter of the National Organization for Women (NOW) in 1970. She went on to join local women in pushing for equal job opportunities, equal pay, and other rights.

In the late 20th century, more and more banks and other businesses headquartered in Delaware.

The busy Market Street Mall in Wilmington

was designed to attract banks to locate their headquarters in the state. The act was especially helpful to banks that issued credit cards. Several large banks did move to Delaware and put up big office buildings in downtown Wilmington. One bank, MBNA (Maryland Bank, National Association), rivaled DuPont as Delaware's largest commercial employer. In 2006, MBNA was acquired by Bank of America.

Toward the end of the 20th century, Delaware's political life reflected the state's diversity. Shien Biau Woo, a Chinese American physics professor at the University of Delaware, was elected lieutenant governor in 1984. He became the highest-ranking Asian American official in the United States. In 1994, Margaret Rose Henry became the first African American woman to serve in Delaware's state senate. And in 2000, Ruth Ann Minner was elected Delaware's first woman governor.

Offshore Wind Farms

THINK ABOUT IT!

PRO

Delaware is considering building a "wind farm" offshore, with windmills that generate electricity through wind power. Many Delawareans believe this will be cheaper and keep the air cleaner than traditional coal burning.

"I would love to see all those windmills out there . . . because it would mean we were moving away from **global warming** and we were doing something progressive and something for the future generations."
—Kit Zak, founder of
Citizens for Clean Power, 2007

CON

Delmarva Power, the company that provides Delaware's electricity, opposes the wind farm. The company believes that the project is too expensive and that the state has not considered other clean energy sources such as solar power.

"Before we rush into a 25-year contract, requiring our customers to pay over $22 billion, we must take the time to do this right. . . . [W]e don't believe it's wise to spend billions of dollars for one source of power without first looking at the alternative choices . . . , which we know can cost a small fraction of what this project will cost."
—Gary Stockbridge, president of
Delmarva Power, 2007

Delaware's economy continues to grow in the 21st century. Growth did not always go smoothly, though. As cities and suburbs expanded into rural areas, they took over more and more open land. Some housing developers wanted to build along fragile coastal areas, which environmentalists wanted to protect. Meanwhile, as the population expanded, many people were concerned about pollution. Some wanted to begin using cleaner—and cheaper—energy sources than coal and oil, such as wind or solar power. Businesspeople, environmentalists, and the government hope to resolve these issues while protecting the interests of all.

WORD TO KNOW

global warming *the gradual warming of the entire planet brought about by increasing air pollution; some experts predict violent weather changes as one consequence*

66

READ
ABOUT

A crowd at
Rehoboth Beach

CHAPTER SIX

PEPPLE

★

THROUGHOUT THE YEARS, PEOPLE FROM ALL OVER THE WORLD HAVE MADE THEIR HOMES IN DELAWARE. They brought their traditions with them, invented new traditions in their new surroundings, or created a blend of old and new. This is reflected in everything from traditional crafts such as wood carving to sports such as punkin chunkin!

UPSTATE AND DOWNSTATE

Delawareans say their state has two regional cultures. One is the culture "above the canal"—that is, north of the Chesapeake and Delaware Canal. This area is small geographically, but Wilmington, the state's largest city, is here. The state's business and industrial centers are in the north, and northern Delawareans tend to have more urban lifestyles. About two-thirds of Delaware's population lives in this region.

South of the canal is lower Delaware—humorously called Slower Lower—or just downstate. It consists of southern New Castle County and all of Kent and Sussex counties. (Some people say Slower Lower is Sussex County alone.) Lower Delaware does include Dover, the capital, and busy resort towns along the shore. But most of downstate Delaware is rural, with chicken and potato farms and small towns where life is slower paced than in the north.

A man in Harrington repaints an American flag on the roof of his barn.

Where Delawareans Live

The colors on this map indicate population density throughout the state.
The darker the color, the more people live there.

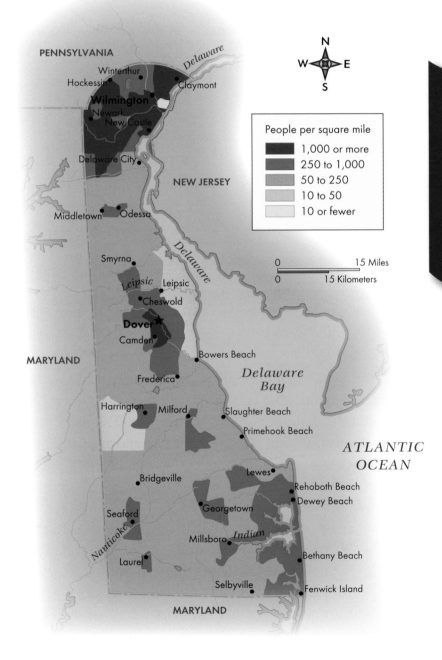

People per square mile

- 1,000 or more
- 250 to 1,000
- 50 to 250
- 10 to 50
- 10 or fewer

0   15 Miles
0   15 Kilometers

FAQ

Q: **HOW MANY STATES HAVE A SMALLER POPULATION THAN DELAWARE?**

A: Only five states have fewer residents—South Dakota, Alaska, North Dakota, Vermont, and Wyoming.

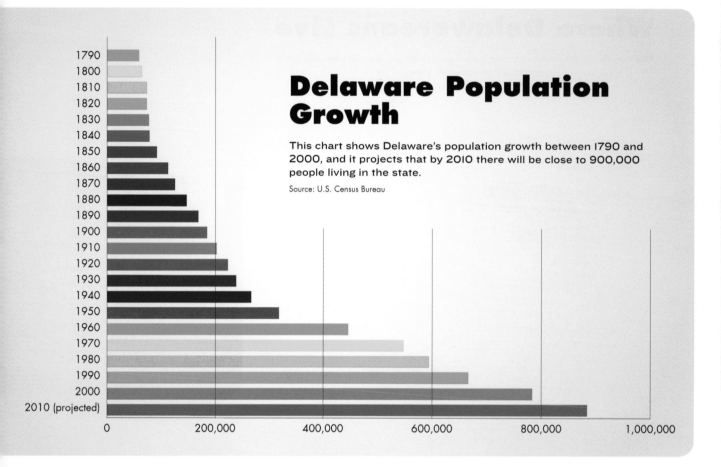

Delaware Population Growth

This chart shows Delaware's population growth between 1790 and 2000, and it projects that by 2010 there will be close to 900,000 people living in the state.

Source: U.S. Census Bureau

Big City Life

This list shows the population of Delaware's biggest cities.

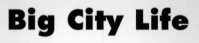

Wilmington	.72,826
Dover	.34,735
Newark	.30,014
Milford	.7,852
Seaford	.7,080

Source: U.S. Census Bureau, 2006 estimate

Delaware has a small population. In 2007, it was home to about 865,000 people. Even Delaware's big cities are small. According to the 2000 census, only Wilmington, Dover, and Newark had more than 20,000 residents.

DELAWARE DIVERSITY

Delawareans come from many backgrounds. According to the 2000 census, about one out of five residents is black. African Americans have a long history in Delaware. Prior to the Civil War, the state was home to a large number of free African Americans as well as to

A crowd takes in folk music at the Big August Quarterly in Wilmington.

some who were enslaved. African Americans have celebrated the Big August Quarterly in Wilmington since 1814. It began as a convention of the African Union Church, when enslaved and free blacks came together to celebrate their faith. It's still a joyous religious festival, with music, dance, food, and exhibits on African American history.

Among Delawareans of European descent, one out of six traced their ancestors to Ireland and one out of seven to Germany. One out of eight people reported English ancestors, and one out of eleven claimed an Italian background. Many Italian immigrants settled in Wilmington in the 1800s. Today, you can still stroll along the brick sidewalks in Wilmington's Little Italy neighborhood and smell delicious aromas from its

Kids watch a parade during a Puerto Rican festival in Wilmington.

SEE IT HERE!

CELEBRATING ITALY

The Italian Festival is one of Delaware's biggest ethnic celebrations. It began in the 1920s in Wilmington's Little Italy neighborhood. Saint Anthony's Roman Catholic Church held the event to honor Saint Anthony of Padua on his feast day, June 13. Today, it has grown to a weeklong festival featuring Italian music, cooking demonstrations, rides, and plenty of Italian food. Keeping to the festival's religious roots, it includes the Procession of Saints, honoring 12 saints important to church members.

bakeries and restaurants. Wilmington's Italian Americans offer up some old traditions at the weeklong Italian Festival in June.

Other Delawareans originate from countries in Eastern Europe such as Poland and Ukraine, Asian lands such as India and China, Middle Eastern countries such as Egypt, and Spanish-speaking lands such as Mexico, Guatemala, and Cuba.

Today, immigrants are still finding new homes in Delaware. In the early 2000s, the greatest number of immigrants in Delaware had come from India, Mexico, China, and the Philippines.

Although most Lenapes and Nanticokes died or were pushed out of Delaware after Europeans arrived in the region, today a small number of Delawareans are Native Americans. The Nanticoke Indian Powwow in Millsboro is an annual homecoming event for Native Americans in the Delaware and New Jersey areas. At the powwow, Nanticokes celebrate their culture and heritage with friends and family through traditional music, dance, storytelling, foods, and crafts.

There is an Amish community in Kent County, just west of Dover. The Amish are a Christian group devoted to a simple life of hard work, charity, and worship. They wear modest clothing, use no electricity, and travel by horse and buggy. Most Amish people live by farming. They grow vegetables, wheat, and corn. Some operate repair shops, woodworking studios, or restaurants serving delicious homemade foods. Handmade Amish furniture, quilts, and other household goods are prized for their fine quality.

Delaware's Amish community is shrinking though. Traffic in the area where they live is increasing, making it dangerous to drive buggies. Land developers are offering extravagant prices to buy Amish farmland. As

FAQ

Q8 HOW MANY NANTICOKES AND LENAPES LIVE IN DELAWARE?

A8 Delaware was home to an estimated 1,000 Nanticokes and 700 to 800 Lenapes in 2007.

Amish farmers talk with each other during an auction in Dover.

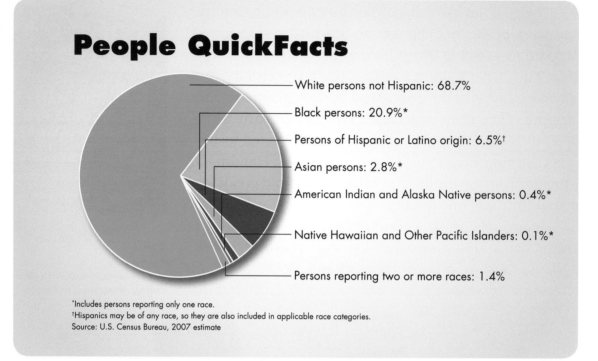

People QuickFacts

White persons not Hispanic: 68.7%

Black persons: 20.9%*

Persons of Hispanic or Latino origin: 6.5%†

Asian persons: 2.8%*

American Indian and Alaska Native persons: 0.4%*

Native Hawaiian and Other Pacific Islanders: 0.1%*

Persons reporting two or more races: 1.4%

*Includes persons reporting only one race.
†Hispanics may be of any race, so they are also included in applicable race categories.
Source: U.S. Census Bureau, 2007 estimate

a result, many Amish families are leaving Delaware to settle in quieter, less-populated parts of the country. As Dover's suburbs expand, many other rural farmers in Kent County are also feeling the pressure of increased population.

EDUCATION

Dutch and Swedish colonists opened Delaware's earliest schools in the 1600s. Most of these schools were operated by churches. English colonists later opened schools of their own. Delaware first set up a public school system in 1829. Today, kids in Delaware are required to attend school from ages 5 through 16. About one-fifth of the state's students attend private schools.

Delaware's first college was Newark College, founded in Newark in 1833. Eventually, that school

Students on a University of Delaware campus

grew into the main campus of Delaware's largest university, the University of Delaware (UD). Other campuses are in Dover, Wilmington, Lewes, and Georgetown. UD has strong programs in agriculture, urban studies, and engineering and other sciences. Delaware State University opened in Dover in 1891 as a college for African American students.

HOW TO TALK LIKE A DELAWAREAN

Do you ever get salty? To some Delawareans, that means angry. When you hear a joke, do you start bagging up? If you're from Delaware, that means laughing a lot. When Delawareans get thirsty, they ask for a soda rather than a pop. If they want a sandwich on a long roll, they order a sub—short for submarine sandwich. Their neighbors in Philadelphia and southern New Jersey call it a hoagie.

HOW TO EAT LIKE A DELAWAREAN

Thanks to their long coastline, Delawareans get to enjoy lots of fresh seafood. Crab is a favorite. It's served steamed, or as crab cakes, crab salad, crab dip, or crabmeat spread. People may use a crab mixture to stuff tomatoes or mushrooms.

Other delicious seafood found in Delaware includes lobster, shrimp, mussels, clams, scallops, Delaware Bay oysters, and many kinds of fresh fish. These are sometimes served in seafood chowder, stew, or bisque, a rich, creamy soup with chunks of seafood.

Locally grown fruits are favorites, too. Peaches, the state fruit, are made into peach butter, peach cobbler, peach tarts, and peach cake and pie.

Blue crab

MENU

WHAT'S ON THE MENU IN DELAWARE?

★ ★ ★

Saltwater taffy

Crab cakes

An authentic Delaware crab cake must use the meat of the blue crab. People make crab cakes many different ways. The cakes can be round or patty-shaped. They can be deep-fried in oil, pan-fried in a skillet, or baked in the oven. They can be mixed with bread crumbs, cracker crumbs, or no crumbs at all.

Slippery dumplings

Slippery dumplings are noodlelike dumplings made from long, flat strips of dough that are dropped into boiling water. They're not to be confused with drop dumplings, which are made from round lumps of dough. Slippery dumplings are usually served in a chicken-and-dumpling dish. In Delaware, chicken with slippery dumplings is often called chicken pot pie. Why are the dumplings slippery? Because, being long and flat, they can absorb more chicken fat than round dumplings!

Scrapple

Scrapple is a specialty food in Delaware. Some Delawareans love it, and some hate it. It's made of pork parts mixed with cornmeal and spices. The mixture is compressed into a loaf. Then slices are fried and served as a breakfast food or eaten in a sandwich. Some people eat scrapple with ketchup or maple syrup on top.

Scrapple

Saltwater taffy

Visitors to Delaware's beaches head straight for the saltwater taffy stands. This sticky, chewy, old-fashioned candy has been a favorite treat for beachgoers for more than 100 years. It's available in many delicious flavors, from peanut butter to peppermint.

TRY THIS RECIPE
Delaware Crab Puffs

These fluffy snacks are a Delaware favorite. Be sure to have an adult nearby to help with the cooking.

Ingredients:
2 cups flour
1 tablespoon baking powder
½ teaspoon salt
1 egg
1 cup milk
½ pound crabmeat
Vegetable oil

Instructions:
1. Mix the flour, baking powder, and salt in a bowl.
2. In a separate bowl, beat the egg.
3. Add the milk and crabmeat to the egg.
4. Stir the wet mixture into the flour mixture, and mix well.
5. Pour enough vegetable oil into a skillet to reach about ¼ inch (0.6 cm) deep.
6. Heat the oil to 375°F.
7. Drop the crab mixture by spoonfuls into the hot oil, and fry until lightly browned. Enjoy!

MINI-BIO

HOWARD PYLE: ILLUSTRATOR

Howard Pyle (1853–1911) was born in Wilmington, where his father had a leather business. As a child, he loved roaming the gardens of his family's home outside Wilmington. Similar gardens appeared in his vivid illustrations in children's books such as *The Merry Adventures of Robin Hood, Howard Pyle's Book of Pirates,* and a four-volume set of books on King Arthur. Later, Pyle established art schools in Wilmington and in Chadds Ford, Pennsylvania. He is sometimes called the Father of American Illustration.

 Want to know more? See www.library.pitt.edu/libraries/is/enroom/illustrators/pyle.htm

ARTISTS, MUSICIANS, AND WRITERS

Many artists and illustrators have found inspiration in the Delaware landscape. Howard Pyle (1853–1911) was an artist who taught in Wilmington. He made dramatic and colorful illustrations of classic children's stories. One of Pyle's students in Wilmington was N. C. Wyeth (1882–1945). He became a book illustrator as well as a painter. Wyeth's son Andrew (1917–) and grandson Jamie (1946–) also became artists. They have lived and worked in the Wilmington area and in nearby Chadds Ford,

Andrew Wyeth was one of the best-known American painters of the 20th century.

Jazz trumpeter Clifford Brown was a highly regarded musician from Wilmington.

Pennsylvania. All three Wyeths painted scenes in the Brandywine Valley. Many of their works are on display in Wilmington's Delaware Art Museum.

Clifford Brown (1930–1956) of Wilmington was a jazz trumpeter who influenced many other jazz musicians of the 1950s. Jazz remains popular in Delaware. At Bethany Beach, summer ends with the Bethany Beach Jazz Festival and the Jazz Funeral. The Jazz Funeral, a mournful parade of musicians, is based on an African American cultural tradition in New Orleans, Louisiana. Jazz musicians slowly march down the seaside boardwalk as spectators "mourn" the passing of summer.

LARA M. ZEISES: YOUNG-ADULT NOVELIST

When she was three, Lara M. Zeises (1976–) moved to Delaware with her family. When she was eight, she enjoyed writing mystery stories on her mother's typewriter. Zeises attended the University of Delaware. She hoped to write TV shows but began writing novels for young adults instead. Her books—which include *Bringing Up the Bones*, *Contents under Pressure*, and *Anyone but You*—deal with the struggles and challenges of being a teenager. Many of her novels take place in Delaware. She teaches at the University of Delaware and gives writing workshops around the country.

Want to know more? See www.zeisgeist.com

Members of Sankofa African Dance and Drum Company performing at a fair in New York

Wilmington is home to the Delaware Symphony Orchestra, Opera Delaware, and the Wilmington Music School. Sankofa African Dance and Drum Company is based in Dover. It teaches African dances and drum rhythms to young people who perform in Delaware and nearby states.

Delaware has produced many successful authors. Mark E. Rogers (1952–) of Newark wrote and illustrated the Samurai Cat books. These humorous fantasy novels present the adventures of a Japanese warrior cat. Another Delaware author, Lara M. Zeises (1976–), has written several award-winning young-adult novels.

Novelist Christopher Castellani grew up in Wilmington.

Christopher Castellani (1972–) grew up in Wilmington, the son of Italian immigrants. His novel *The Saint of Lost Things* portrays the Italian immigrant experience in Wilmington. Colleen Faulkner (1962?–) is a Delaware author who writes historical romances and suspense novels under the names Hunter Morgan and V. K. Forrest. Many of her stories are set in Delaware.

TRADITIONAL ARTS AND CRAFTS

Craftspeople in Delaware draw on many traditions to create both useful and decorative pieces of art. Carving waterbirds out of wood is a traditional folk art in Delaware and other regions along the Atlantic coast. Wood-carvers make lifelike models of geese, swans, and shorebirds such as herons and egrets.

Carving duck decoys is a specialized craft. Decoys are models of mallards, pintails, and other duck species. Duck hunters put them in the water to lure live ducks. One of the nation's most respected decoy artists was Ira Hudson (1873–1949), who grew up near Williamsville in Sussex County. Collectors pay high prices for his expertly crafted decoys. Today, most decoy carvers make them as a decorative art, rather than for use in hunting.

Many crafts grew out of Delaware's shipbuilding and sailing traditions. For example, some wood-carvers make model boats and ships. Others carve wooden lighthouses, including models of lighthouses along Delaware's coast. Delaware wood-carvers also make walking canes, birdhouses, and furniture.

Some Delaware artists make sculptures out of driftwood, which is wood that has washed up on the beaches and shores. Tossed in the waves and storms for years, these pieces of wood are rough, jagged, and strangely beautiful.

Many Delaware craftspeople are known for making specialized duck decoys.

The work of a Delaware quilter

Women in Delaware have passed down the art of quilt making since colonial times. In the early days, they used scraps of cloth or cut pieces of old clothes. They sewed the pieces together to make a big rectangle, added a backing, and stuffed the quilt with feathers to make it warm. Sometimes several women in a village would meet for a quilting bee to work on a quilt together.

During the days of slavery, African American women made quilts with designs that contained secret codes for slaves escaping to freedom. The women would hang the quilts outside so escapees could find directions or learn some important news. For example, a wagon wheel meant it was time to start traveling. A flying-geese design pointed the way to Canada, and a bear paw pointed the way to reach food and water. Teresa Barkley, a modern quilt maker from Delaware, uses unusual materials to tell detailed stories in her work.

WHITTLING MAN

When he was just eight years old, Jehu Camper (1897–1989) started **whittling** wood on his Harrington farm. He whittled little windmills and put them all around the farm. As he grew older, he wanted to preserve his memories of old-fashioned farm days. So he began whittling figures to create elaborate farm scenes. They depicted activities such as milking cows, grinding corn, and making horseshoes. Camper's scenes are displayed in the "Whittlin' History" exhibit at Dover's Delaware Agricultural Museum and Village.

WORD TO KNOW

whittling *carving wood using only a small, light knife; usually done as a hobby*

Fans watch a race at the Dover International Speedway.

SPORTS

Delaware has no professional sports teams. Many sports fans in the state root for teams based in nearby cities such as Baltimore, Philadelphia, and Washington, D.C. They also come out to cheer for the Wilmington Blue Rocks, a minor league baseball team that plays on Judy Johnson Field in Wilmington's Riverfront district.

The University of Delaware's Fightin' Blue Hens football team draws both local and out-of-state fans. More than 20,000 Blue Hens fans fill Newark's Delaware Stadium for home games. A big blue-and-gold hen named YoUDee is the team's mascot.

Horse racing is a popular sport in Delaware. Thousands of racing fans come to the Dover Downs racetrack in Dover and to the Delaware Park racetrack in Stanton. Dover Downs specializes in harness racing. That involves a horse pulling a two-wheeled cart with a driver. Delaware Park is a **thoroughbred** horse-racing track.

WORD TO KNOW

thoroughbred *a horse carefully bred for generations to be a racing horse*

Even more people flock to the Dover International Speedway, which hosts NASCAR (National Association for Stock Car Auto Racing) races. The speedway's 1-mile (1.6 km) track is paved with concrete instead of asphalt, which most NASCAR tracks have. Because the concrete track is so hard on cars, it's called the Monster Mile. A giant, concrete monster is the speedway's mascot.

Punkin chunkin—or pumpkin chucking—is an unusual sport that began in Delaware. The World Championship Punkin Chunkin takes place in Sussex County every fall. Contestants use massive machines to hurl pumpkins as far as they can. Some people launch their pumpkins with air cannons. But most launching devices are old types of machines used in warfare such as **catapults**. Would you like to try chunkin a punkin? Come on down. There are punkin chunkin divisions for kids, too!

MINI-BIO

WILLIAM "JUDY" JOHNSON: BASEBALL HALL OF FAMER

Born in Maryland, William Julius Johnson (1899–1989) moved to Wilmington's west side with his family when he was five. He loved baseball, but his father wanted him to become a boxer, warning his son that an African American baseball player couldn't go far. But Johnson was determined. At the time, African Americans weren't allowed to play in the Major Leagues, so he joined the Negro Leagues. He became a star batter and third baseman for the Hilldale Daisies, the Homestead Grays, and the Pittsburgh Crawfords, all Pennsylvania teams. In 1975, he became the first Delawarean ever inducted into the National Baseball Hall of Fame.

? Want to know more? See www.hsd.org/DHE/ DHE_who_johnson.htm

WORD TO KNOW

catapults *machines with a long, wooden arm used to fling stones or other objects against or over walls*

As of 2007, the record distance for a pumpkin hurled in the Punkin Chunkin was 4,434 feet (1,351 m). That's about five-sixths of a mile! The record was set by a compressed-air cannon in 2003.

READ ABOUT

Visitors explore
the grounds at
Legislative Hall.

CHAPTER SEVEN

DECEMBER 7, 1787

GOVERNMENT

★

DELAWARE GOVERNMENT ISN'T JUST FOR GROWN-UPS. Kids get involved, too. Elementary school students all over the state had a strong voice in choosing several of Delaware's official state symbols. They did research, held discussions, and voted in their classrooms. Then they wrote letters to their state lawmakers. Those letters persuaded lawmakers to adopt the students' proposals. The lawmakers approved the peach blossom as the state flower, the ladybug as the state bug, the tiger swallowtail as the state butterfly, and belemnite as the state fossil.

Legislative Hall in Dover

THE CAPITAL AND THE CONSTITUTION

Dover has been Delaware's capital city since 1777. New Castle was the capital before that. Most of the important state government offices are located in Dover.

First State Heritage Park stretches out along grassy lawns in downtown Dover and links some of Delaware's most important government and historical sites. It includes Legislative Mall, whose centerpiece is Legislative Hall, the state capitol. The building is topped by a cupola tower, or tower with a small dome, and a weathervane that shows the wind's direction. Displayed on the grounds in front of the capitol is a replica of the Liberty Bell in Philadelphia, Pennsylvania. On the Green

Capitol Facts

Here are some fascinating facts about Delaware's state capitol.

Exterior height: 90 feet (27 m)
On top: A cupola tower with a weathervane
Number of stories high: 2, plus a basement
Paintings displayed: Former governors and Delaware World War II heroes
Surrounding grounds: Legislative Mall
Location: 411 Legislative Avenue, Dover
Construction dates: 1931–1933; north and south wings added 1965–1970; east wings added 1994

Capital City

This map shows places of interest in Dover, Delaware's capital city.

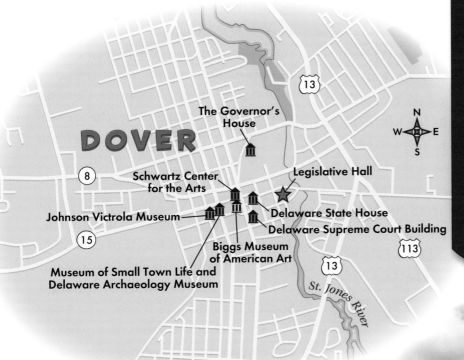

DOVER

The Governor's House

Legislative Hall

Schwartz Center for the Arts

Johnson Victrola Museum

Delaware State House

Delaware Supreme Court Building

Biggs Museum of American Art

Museum of Small Town Life and Delaware Archaeology Museum

St. Jones River

FAQ

Q: WHAT'S THAT BIG CUBE WEST OF THE GREEN IN DOVER?

A: Located in Constitution Park, it's a huge stone cube with the U.S. Constitution inscribed on it. This honors Delaware's status as the first state to ratify the Constitution. Atop the cube is a 12-foot (3.7 m) bronze quill. Quills are big feathers that were used as writing pens in the 1700s.

nearby are historical buildings such as the Delaware State House, Kent County Courthouse, and the Delaware Supreme Court Building.

Delaware's current state constitution was adopted in 1897. It has been updated with many new amendments since then. The constitution outlines Delaware's basic form of government. Like the U.S. Constitution, it provides for three branches of state government—executive, legislative, and judicial.

SEE IT HERE!

FIRST SATURDAYS

First Saturdays in the First State—the first Saturday of every month—are great times to visit First State Heritage Park. That's when each site at the park holds special programs and events for visitors, including guided tours of Legislative Hall. Events often revolve around a theme such as colonial life or Civil War days. One First Saturday, for example, celebrated women's lives in historic times. A costumed guide posed the question, "What would your life be like if you were a housewife in 1862?" The program covered lifestyle, as well as fashion, career choices, and health issues.

RUTH ANN MINNER: GROUNDBREAKING GOVERNOR

Ruth Ann Minner (1935—) was born in Slaughter Neck, in Sussex County. She had to leave school at age 16 to help out on the family farm. After her first husband died, she worked hard to support her three sons. She eventually became a clerk in the Delaware House of Representatives and then, in 1974, a member of the house itself. In 2000, she was elected Delaware's first female governor. As governor, she has promoted education, health care, and environmental protection.

? **Want to know more?** See http://governor.delaware.gov/biography.shtml

THE EXECUTIVE BRANCH

Delaware's governor is the head of the executive branch of government. The governor is elected to a four-year term and may serve for only two terms. His or her responsibilities include approving or rejecting bills passed by the Delaware General Assembly, commanding the state's National Guard troops, and directing emergency responses to disasters such as extreme weather. The governor also appoints most judges and other important government officials. These include the heads of executive departments such as the Department of Finance and Delaware Health and Social Services.

Several other executive officials are elected to four-year terms. They include the lieutenant governor, who assists the governor and takes his or her place if necessary; the attorney general, who handles the state's legal affairs; the insurance commissioner, who oversees the state's insurance companies; the treasurer, who receives and manages state income such as taxes; and the auditor of accounts, who reviews financial operations of state and local governments.

THE LEGISLATIVE BRANCH

The Delaware General Assembly is Delaware's legislature, or lawmaking body. Its job is to make state laws. When assembly members are considering a new law, they debate its good and bad points. Assembly

Delaware's State Government

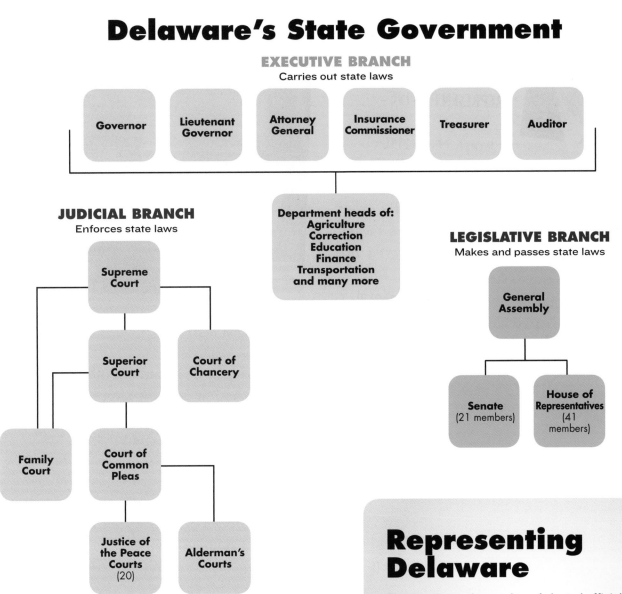

EXECUTIVE BRANCH
Carries out state laws

Governor | Lieutenant Governor | Attorney General | Insurance Commissioner | Treasurer | Auditor

Department heads of:
**Agriculture
Correction
Education
Finance
Transportation
and many more**

JUDICIAL BRANCH
Enforces state laws

Supreme Court
Superior Court
Court of Chancery
Family Court
Court of Common Pleas
Justice of the Peace Courts (20)
Alderman's Courts

LEGISLATIVE BRANCH
Makes and passes state laws

General Assembly
Senate (21 members)
House of Representatives (41 members)

Representing Delaware

This list shows the number of elected officials who represent Delaware, both on the state and national levels.

OFFICE	NUMBER	LENGTH OF TERM
State senators	21	4 years
State representatives	41	2 years
U.S. senators	2	6 years
U.S. representatives	1	2 years
Presidential electors	3	—

members belong to special committees such as agriculture, education, and the environment. Committee members, or the whole General Assembly, may call in experts or ordinary citizens to give arguments on each side of an issue. They answer questions such

JOSEPH MIRÓ: FROM REFUGEE TO REPRESENTATIVE

Joseph Miró (1946–) was born in Cuba and arrived in Wilmington when he was a teenager. He was a refugee fleeing Cuba, which had recently experienced a revolution. After college, Miró taught school for 31 years. In 1998, he was elected to the Delaware House of Representatives, becoming the first Hispanic member of the General Assembly. Inspired by his teaching experience, he focused on improving education in the state. Never forgetting his Cuban roots and the difficulties of adjusting to a new country, he remains active in Delaware's Hispanic community.

? Want to know more? See www.nhcsl.org/news/nov16-2007.html

Governor Minner addresses the state legislature in 2005.

as why a new road should be built or whether a new shopping mall will have a sufficient water supply.

The General Assembly is made up of two houses. One is the house of representatives, with 41 members. The other is the senate, with 21 members. They all meet in Dover's Legislative Hall, a building also known as the state capitol. Voters elect representatives to two-year terms and senators to four-year terms.

THE JUDICIAL BRANCH

The judicial branch of Delaware's government is made up of judges and their courts. Their job is to apply the law and determine if laws have been broken.

The Court of Chancery handles disputes between corporations. This is important in Delaware, where so many corporations are headquartered. The court has five judges—a chancellor and four vice chancellors. The Court of Chancery does not hold jury trials. Instead, one chancellor hears each case and makes a decision.

The Delaware Supreme Court is the state's highest court. It consists of a chief justice, or judge, and four associate justices. The supreme court hears appeals from lower courts. That is, if someone disagrees with a lower court's decision, he or she can appeal to the supreme court to review the decision.

The Superior Court of Delaware is below the supreme court. It presides over jury trials involving serious

Reporters wait for trial results outside the Court of Chancery in Georgetown.

MINI-BIO

JOSEPH BIDEN JR.: STRONG VOICE IN THE SENATE

Born in Pennsylvania, Joseph R. Biden Jr. (1942–) moved with his family to New Castle County when he was 10. He was first elected to the U.S. Senate in 1972 and eventually became the longest-serving senator in Delaware's history. He has been a strong voice in Congress, serving as chairman of both the Senate Judiciary Committee and the Senate Foreign Relations Committee. He has advocated drug control and been a strong supporter of Delaware industry. In 2008, Biden was selected as Barack Obama's running mate in the presidential election.

 Want to know more? See http://bioguide.congress.gov/scripts/biodisplay.pl?index=B000444

WEIRD AND WACKY LAWS

Delaware has some pretty wacky laws that remain on the books. Do you think these are still enforced?

- It's illegal to fly over any body of water unless you are carrying sufficient supplies of food and drink.
- It's against the law to whisper in church in Rehoboth Beach.
- In Lewes, it's illegal to wear pants that are "form-fitting" around the waist.

BURYING THE HATCHET

Citizens in Georgetown have a unique ritual at election time. They celebrate Return Day on the Thursday after the November elections. This tradition recalls the 1700s, when rural residents traveled to Georgetown to vote in elections, which were held on Tuesday. Then they'd wait until Thursday to hear the results, or returns.

Today, the town crier reads election results from the courthouse balcony. Then, dressed in old-time finery, the winners and losers of the elections ride together in a horse-drawn carriage to the town circle. Following a custom of local Native Americans, the former political rivals bury a hatchet in the sand to symbolize the end of rivalry and the beginning of a new friendship.

cases. Delaware's family courts handle family and child-custody cases. The Court of Common Pleas deals with minor legal cases.

Judges in all of these courts serve 12-year terms. They are appointed by the governor and approved by the state senate.

LOCAL GOVERNMENT

Delaware is divided into three counties—New Castle, Kent, and Sussex. In New Castle County, voters elect a 13-member council, a council president, and a county executive. In Sussex County, voters elect a five-member council, with one member serving as president. Kent County has a seven-member board of commissioners called the levy court. Counties also elect a sheriff, a comptroller (who keeps track of the county's money), and a recorder of deeds (property).

Most of Delaware's cities and towns are governed by a city council and a mayor or city manager. Smaller communities are classed as villages, and many small, rural communities are called unincorporated places. Three of Delaware's six largest "cities" are actually unincorporated places—Pike Creek, Bear, and Brookside.

Each county in Delaware is divided into units called hundreds. This is a practice left over from old English times, when it was used to determine taxes. William Penn first divided Delaware into hundreds in 1682. Borders have changed, but the basic practice remains. Today, however, hundreds aren't used for governing or taxation. They are mostly used to indicate property locations. Several eastern states were divided into hundreds in colonial times. Now Delaware is the only state that still has hundreds. The First State is the last state to keep this old tradition.

Delaware Counties

This map shows the three counties in Delaware. Dover, the state capital, is indicated with a star.

Delaware, with 3 counties, has the fewest counties of any state in the nation. Texas has the most, with 254!

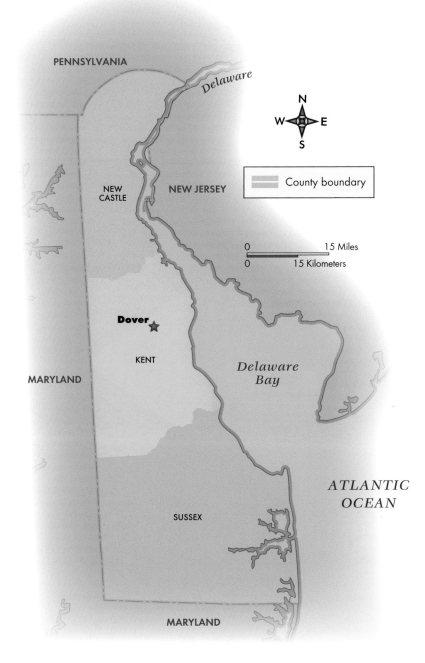

State Flag

The state flag of Delaware was adopted on July 24, 1913. It features part of the state seal of Delaware in the center of a buff-colored diamond. The diamond is surrounded by a shade of blue called colonial blue. At the bottom of the flag, the date of statehood for Delaware, December 7, 1787, is displayed. It has been said that the flag's colonial blue and buff colors represent the colors that General George Washington wore during the Revolutionary War.

State Seal

The state seal of Delaware contains several symbols that represent the state's economy and history. The seal features a sheaf of wheat and a farmer holding his hoe, symbolizing Delaware's agricultural strength. Near the center of the seal is an ox, which represents the importance of livestock to the state's economy. On the right side of the seal stands a musketeer, representing the brave citizens who have taken up arms to defend the state of Delaware over the years. Below the farmer and the musketeer is a ribbon displaying the state's motto, "Liberty and Independence."

At the bottom of the seal are three dates representing milestones in Delaware's history: 1704, the year that Delaware formed its first assembly; 1776, the year of independence for the United States; and 1787, the year in which Delaware ratified the U.S. Constitution and became the first state. The first seal was adopted on January 17, 1777. The current version was adopted in 2004.

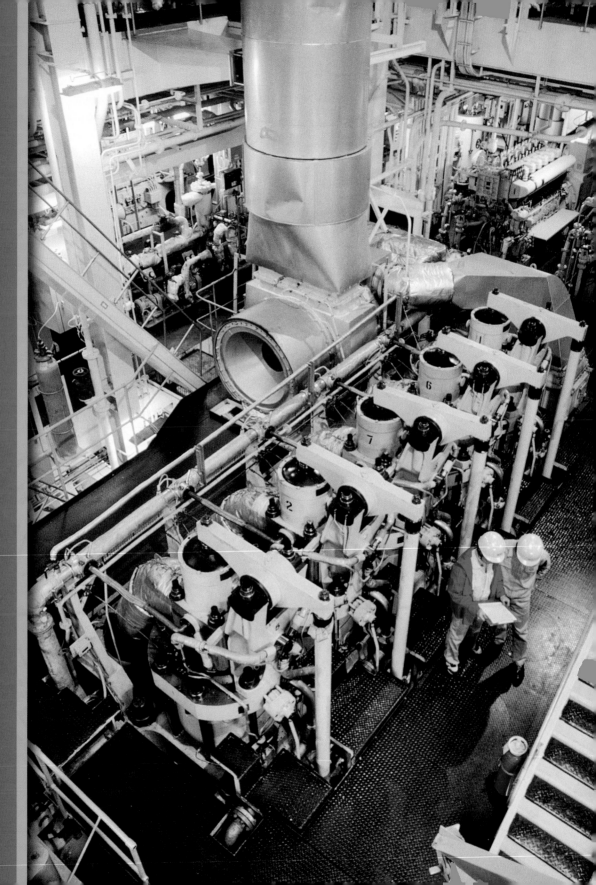

98

READ ABOUT

Workers produce
ship engines in a
Delaware factory.

CHAPTER EIGHT

ECONOMY

★

DELAWARE HAS A BOOMING ECONOMY. If someone in your family uses a credit card, it's likely that the payments are processed in Delaware. If you wear a nylon jacket or use a toothbrush, you are using products developed in Delaware. Chickens, milk, and crabs are some of the state's other leading products. You'll find Delaware goods in homes and businesses all over the world.

Visitors enjoy the sights and shopping at Bethany Beach.

WORD TO KNOW

incorporate *to register as a company under the laws of a local, state, or national government*

CORPORATIONS AND TAXES

Two big issues stand out in Delaware's economic life. One is taxes. When Delawareans travel out of state, they're always surprised by the sales taxes. Delaware has no state sales tax. If you buy an item that costs $5.00, you pay $5.00 and no more. This makes Delaware an attractive place to shop. People drive in from neighboring states to shop in Delaware.

The other issue is corporations. Delaware's laws are designed to encourage businesses. The state offers them many legal protections and makes it easy to **incorporate** and do business in Delaware. The laws are especially beneficial to banking activities. As a result, hundreds of thousands of companies are registered under Delaware law. Some have their headquarters there, but most do almost all their business

What Do Delawareans Do?

This color-coded chart shows what industries Delawareans work in.

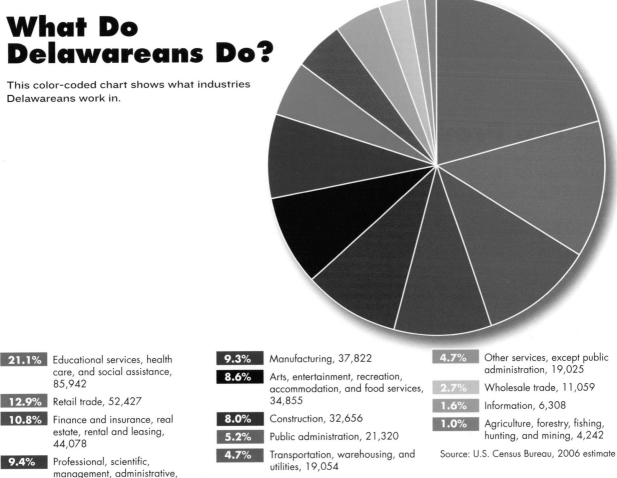

21.1%	Educational services, health care, and social assistance, 85,942
12.9%	Retail trade, 52,427
10.8%	Finance and insurance, real estate, rental and leasing, 44,078
9.4%	Professional, scientific, management, administrative, and waste management services, 38,076

9.3%	Manufacturing, 37,822
8.6%	Arts, entertainment, recreation, accommodation, and food services, 34,855
8.0%	Construction, 32,656
5.2%	Public administration, 21,320
4.7%	Transportation, warehousing, and utilities, 19,054

4.7%	Other services, except public administration, 19,025
2.7%	Wholesale trade, 11,059
1.6%	Information, 6,308
1.0%	Agriculture, forestry, fishing, hunting, and mining, 4,242

Source: U.S. Census Bureau, 2006 estimate

activities outside the state. In fact, more than half of the nation's highest-income corporations are incorporated in Delaware. They include many banks, credit card companies, and other financial institutions.

SERVICE INDUSTRIES

Services are Delaware's number-one industry. Service workers provide people with helpful services, rather than providing goods such as farm products or manufactured items.

Banking and other financial activities are Delaware's leading service industry. Many large banks have their credit card operations in Delaware. That includes Bank of America, the nation's largest bank. Wilmington is a national center for the credit card industry. Many insurance and investment companies have their headquarters in Wilmington, too. All these businesses employ thousands of people.

Other service workers include real estate salespeople, health care workers, lawyers, store clerks, truck drivers, and repair people. Some are government employees. They may work at Dover Air Force Base or teach in public schools.

Top Products

Agriculture	Chickens, corn, milk, soybeans, peas, potatoes
Manufacturing	Chemicals, food products, paper products, automobiles
Fishing	Crabs, clams
Mining	Sand and gravel, magnesium

FAQ

Q: WHAT ARE SOME MATERIALS DEVELOPED BY DUPONT?

A:

Material	Description or Common Uses
Corian	Hard material used for kitchen countertops
Kevlar	Bulletproof vests for law enforcement, sports equipment
Mylar	Food packaging, aerospace equipment
Neoprene	Waterproof clothing, divers' wet suits
Nylon	Fabric, carpeting, rope, toothbrush bristles
Tyvek	Envelopes, coats for lab workers, covering for construction projects

MADE IN DELAWARE

Have you ever had a sandwich wrapped in cellophane? If so, you were using a chemical product made in Delaware. Chemicals are Delaware's leading factory goods. The state's largest chemical company is the DuPont Company. This homegrown company had its start as a gunpowder mill along Brandywine Creek in the 1600s. Today, it's one of the largest chemical companies in the world. DuPont makes hundreds of common **synthetic** materials such as cellophane and nylon. Many of its products have medical or industrial uses, too.

WORD TO KNOW

synthetic *artificial; related to something that doesn't occur in nature*

Major Agricultural and Mining Products

This map shows where Delaware's major agricultural and mining products come from. See a milk carton? That means dairy products are found there.

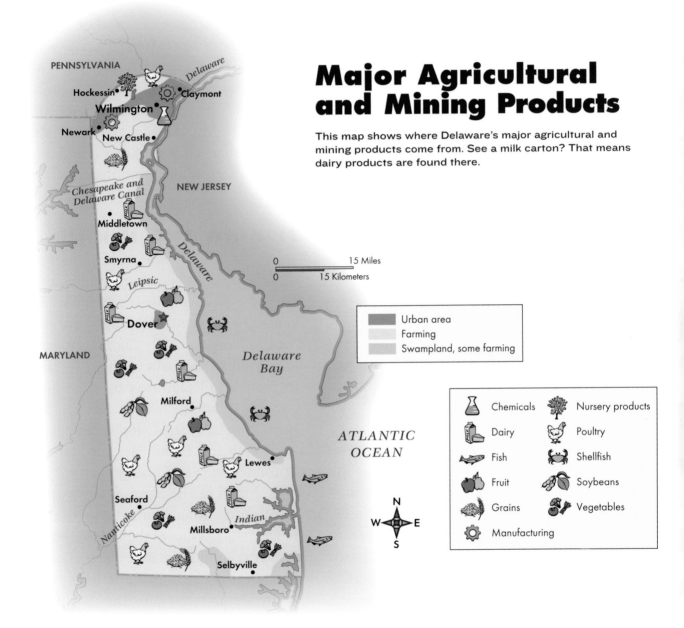

Several other chemical manufacturers are based in Delaware. One is Hercules, which produces chemicals used in making paper. Syngenta manufactures chemicals for the agriculture industry, and AstraZeneca makes medicines.

WALLACE CAROTHERS: INVENTOR

Wallace Carothers (1896–1937) was a brilliant inventor who worked for the DuPont Company from 1928 until his death. As a child in Iowa, he was fascinated with machines and tools and spent hours doing experiments. He went on to become a chemist. DuPont hired him to help develop artificial materials. Carothers and his research team invented neoprene, an artificial rubber, in 1931. When DuPont wanted an artificial silk, Carothers's team invented nylon. Dozens of other new materials emerged under his direction.

? Want to know more? See www.pbs.org/wgbh/aso/databank/entries/btcaro.html

Sussex County produces more chickens than any other county in the nation. The county's farmers raise more than 200 million chickens a year!

Food processing is another important industry in Delaware. Many food plants in Delaware process chickens. Others prepare canned goods, pudding and other desserts, baked goods, and soft drinks. Factories in Delaware also make automobiles, paper products, medical and scientific equipment, and plastic products.

FISHING AND MINING

Every morning, fishers head out in their boats from Lewes and many other coastal towns. Shellfish are especially valuable catches, and crabs are the most valuable of all. Clams, lobsters, and oysters are some other shellfish important to Delaware's fishing industry. The leading fish catches include perch, sea bass, shad, and weakfish.

Delaware ranks last among the states in mineral production. Sand and gravel are the top mining products. Much of the sand is taken from underwater areas offshore. Magnesium is extracted from seawater, and Delaware is one of the leading states in mining magnesium compounds. They are used in making medicines and other chemical products.

One of Delaware's nicknames is the Diamond State, but no diamonds are mined there. The nickname is traced to President Thomas Jefferson. According to legend, he called Delaware a jewel among the states because of its important location along the Atlantic coast. So Delawareans decided their state was not just any jewel, but a diamond!

AGRICULTURE

Drive through Kent and Sussex counties, and you'll see thousands of acres of farmland. Farmers there raise tons of products that go to markets in cities such as Washington, D.C., Philadelphia, Baltimore, and New York City. Although most of the state's farmland is used for crops, most of the farm income comes from livestock. The most valuable farm product is broilers, or young chickens. Farmers in Sussex County raise most of those chickens. This county has many hog farms, too, and farmers in both counties raise dairy cattle. Milk, the state beverage, is the top dairy product.

Corn and soybeans are Delaware's leading crops. Wheat, peas, and potatoes are major crops, too. Many farmers in southern Delaware specialize in growing potatoes. Peaches were once Delaware's leading crop. Today, peaches and apples are important orchard crops. Greenhouse and nursery products are another source of farm income. They include shrubs, flowers, Christmas trees, and other decorative plants.

SEE IT HERE!

HIGHLAND ORCHARDS

Some farms in Delaware grow all their crops without using any chemical pesticides, or insect killers. One is Highland Orchards, a family-owned farm in Wilmington. Its farmers grow fruits such as apples, peaches, strawberries, and raspberries. They use a cider mill to press juice from the apples. Highland Orchards also grows pumpkins, cucumbers, tomatoes, peppers, and corn. On a visit there, you'll see pigs, goats, chickens, and peacocks. You can also shop for fresh foods, local honey, and baked goods.

A Delaware farmer plows a field.

CHAPTER NINE

TRAVEL GUIDE

★

DELAWARE IS A GREAT PLACE TO DISCOVER HISTORY AND NATURE—AND HAVE FUN! You can explore seafaring history, from pirates to shipwrecks. Along the beaches, you can make sand castles, watch wading birds, and even collect coins that wash ashore. The big cities, Wilmington and Dover, are chock-full of fascinating museums and luxurious gardens and parks.

⟵ Follow along with this travel map. We'll begin in Wilmington and go all the way down to Rehoboth Beach.

NEW CASTLE COUNTY

THINGS TO DO: Tour a sailing ship, dress up in costumes from the 1800s, and visit the mill where the DuPont Company began.

Wilmington

★ **Delaware Art Museum:** As you enter this museum, you'll see enormous, colorful glass flowers overhead. Inside are more than 12,000 works of art, including many by the Wyeth family, who spent years in Delaware.

★ **Delaware History Museum:** Use the many interactive exhibits to learn about Delaware and its people from the 1600s to today. Don't miss Grandma's Attic, where you can dress up in old-time clothing and play with historic games and toys.

★ **Nemours Mansion and Gardens:** Set among formal gardens, this French-style mansion was built for Alfred I. du Pont. Its 102 rooms are full of antique furniture, rare rugs, detailed tapestries, and outstanding works of art.

An exhibit at the Delaware Museum of Natural History

★ **Delaware Museum of Natural History:** Here you can explore an African watering hole, marvel at life-size dinosaurs and a giant squid, navigate the Great Barrier Reef, and experience the interactive Discovery Room.

SEE IT HERE!

HAGLEY MUSEUM

Éleuthère Irénée du Pont de Nemours's original gunpowder mills are located on this 235-acre (95 ha) estate, which spreads out along Brandywine Creek in Wilmington. You can tour the du Pont home, see old machines in action, and even try working some machines yourself. In the workers' community, you'll meet costumed guides who demonstrate life in the 1800s. Be sure to visit the schoolhouse, where you can take part in a mid-1800s school day.

★ **Hispanic Festival/El Festival Hispano:** Every September, Wilmington celebrates Hispanic traditions through concerts, dance performances, art exhibits, traditional foods, and children's activities.

★ **Delaware Toy and Miniature Museum:** Check out this huge collection of antique and modern trains, airplanes, boats, games, dolls, dollhouses, and miniature objects.

★ **Bellevue Hall at Bellevue State Park:** This mansion once belonged to William H. du Pont Jr. It is modeled after Montpelier, President James Madison's home in Virginia.

★ **Kalmar Nyckel Shipyard and Museum:** At the waterfront, explore the *Kalmar Nyckel*, an authentic re-creation of one of the ships that brought the first Swedish settlers to Delaware in the 1600s.

★ **Brandywine Zoo:** At Delaware's only zoo, you'll see creatures such as majestic Siberian tigers, playful river otters, colorful macaws, and curious South American tamarin monkeys.

Elephant vase

★ **Fort Christina:** This is where Swedish settlers established Delaware's first permanent European settlement in 1638. You'll learn about their lives as you tour historic buildings such as the Hendrickson House Museum and Old Swedes Church.

Claymont

★ **Howard High School:** This building is a National Historic Landmark because it was one of the schools targeted in the U.S. Supreme Court's 1954 ruling to end racial segregation. It was the first school in Delaware to offer a complete high school education to black students.

SEE IT HERE!

WINTERTHUR MUSEUM AND COUNTRY ESTATE

This is where Henry Francis du Pont began collecting American arts. He had to triple the size of his house to hold all his collections of soup bowls, thimbles, and other objects! Today, you can tour du Pont's 175-room mansion and see his many collections. You can also stroll or take a tram ride around the estate, where you'll see woodlands, meadows, ponds, and many colorful gardens. One popular spot is the Enchanted Woods, a fairy-tale garden with the Tulip Tree House and many other fanciful things to explore.

Greenville

★ **Mount Cuba Center:** This was the 630-acre (255 ha) country estate of Lammot du Pont Copeland. Now it's a garden featuring plants native to the Piedmont region. Visit in the spring and fall, and you'll see spectacular displays of wildflowers.

Newark

★ **Iron Hill Museum:** This building used to be Iron Hill School, a one-room schoolhouse built in 1923 for African American children. It was one of 89 schools Pierre S. du Pont had built for African American children because the state legislature neglected their education.

SEE IT HERE!

OKTOBERFEST

Delaware has a large German American population, and in Newark, German Americans celebrate their heritage with Oktoberfest—which is actually held in September. It's sponsored by the Delaware Saengerbund, German for "singing society." Visitors come to enjoy traditional German music, costumed folk dancing, and delicious German foods such as bratwurst, sauerkraut, German potato salad, and plum cake.

SEE IT HERE!

NEW CASTLE COURT HOUSE MUSEUM

Built in 1732, the New Castle Court House was Delaware's first capitol. On this site in 1776, the Delaware counties declared their independence from Pennsylvania. Here, too, abolitionists Thomas Garrett and John Hunn were found guilty of helping fugitive slaves. Today, exhibits at the museum explore events in Delaware's history, including the history of laws and court cases that affected enslaved and free African Americans.

New Castle

★ **Amstel House:** Built by wealthy landowner John Finney, this house had many important visitors, including George Washington and Delaware's signers of the Declaration of Independence. Tour the home to see colonial arts and crafts such as textiles, furniture, ceramics, and metals, along with photographs and books.

★ **Immanuel Church:** This church was completed in about 1710. George Read, a signer of the Declaration of Independence, and other prominent early Delawareans are buried in its churchyard.

★ **Read House and Gardens:** This grand 22-room house was the largest house in Delaware when it was built in 1801. Today, it is decorated in the style of the time it was built. The current garden, which was planted in 1847, is the oldest surviving garden in the region.

Pea Patch Island

★ **Fort Delaware State Park:** Costumed guides at this historic fort tell you all about the days when thousands of Confederate soldiers were held as prisoners there. To reach the island, you take a ferry from Delaware City.

Visitors at Fort Delaware State Park

★ **Hiking trails:** Wander along the island's hiking trails, and you'll see lots of long-legged herons, egrets, and ibises. This island is one of the largest nesting areas for wading birds on the Atlantic coast.

Heron

Hockessin

★ **Ashland Nature Center:** Stroll along one of four self-guided trails through rolling fields, meadows, woodlands, and marshes. From June through September, the Butterfly House is open. Nearby is a historic covered bridge.

KENT COUNTY

THINGS TO DO: Visit two state capitols, stroll through a farming village, explore 12,000 years of history, and learn how sound recordings began.

Dover

★ **Delaware State House:** This historic building was Delaware's capitol from 1792 to 1933. Take a tour to see the old courtroom and the state legislature's former chambers.

★ **Legislative Hall:** This is where Delaware's General Assembly meets. You can watch lawmakers in action when the legislature is in session.

★ **Delaware Agricultural Museum and Village:** This sprawling, indoor-outdoor museum celebrates Delaware's agricultural heritage with old farm machinery, a log house, dairy cows, and chickens. The 1890s farm village includes a farmhouse, blacksmith shop, store, school, mill, church, train station, and barbershop.

★ **Delaware Archaeology Museum:** Explore 12,000 years of Delaware history through artifacts, exhibits, hands-on activities, and demonstrations. The oldest artifacts date from Delaware's early peoples at the end of the ice age.

SEE IT HERE!

MUSEUM OF SMALL TOWN LIFE

This fascinating museum stands in First State Heritage Park. Here you'll travel back in time for a glimpse into small-town life in Delaware in the late 1800s. Browse through the general store, print shop, drugstore, post office, and woodworking shop. You'll see how ordinary citizens shopped, what they bought, and how little they paid!

Display at the Johnson Victrola Museum

★ **Johnson Victrola Museum:** This museum is dedicated to Delawarean Eldridge Reeves Johnson, who founded the Victor Talking Machine Company in 1901. It was the leading producer of phonograph records in the early 20th century. Exhibits include phonographs, recordings, and other objects related to the history of the sound-recording industry.

★ **John Dickinson Plantation:** Immerse yourself in 1700s life as you mingle and chat with costumed guides. They'll help you explore Dickinson's 1740 mansion, smokehouse, stable, barn, and other buildings. Dickinson was a member of the Continental Congress, the Delaware Assembly, and the Constitutional Convention.

SEE IT HERE!

DELAWARE STATE FAIR

In July, the Delaware State Fair in Harrington, southwest of Frederica, offers 10 days of fun. More than 30,000 people come to see the livestock exhibits, enjoy concerts and games, and sample delicious, homemade foods. Competitions include a rooster-crowing contest, a pretty animal contest, and a table-setting competition!

Frederica

★ **Barratt's Chapel:** This chapel is often called the Cradle of Methodism. Methodist leaders Francis Asbury and Thomas Coke met here in 1784 and began organizing the Methodist Episcopal Church in America.

Near Leipsic

★ **Bombay Hook National Wildlife Refuge:** Every year, about 170,000 people visit this refuge, which covers thousands of acres of marshes, meadows, pools, and forestlands. For waterbirds and other wildlife, it's a safe refuge and breeding ground.

SUSSEX COUNTY

THINGS TO DO: Stroll across sandy beaches, enjoy wildlife along the shore, learn about the Nanticoke people, or inspect the treasure from shipwrecks.

Millsboro

★ **Nanticoke Indian Museum:** This museum tells the history of Delaware's Nanticoke people through their clothing, tools, and other goods. It also holds an extensive Native American library.

★ **Festival Hispano:** This August festival honors a different Latin American country every year, with traditional music, dancing, and foods.

Bridgeville

★ **Apple-Scrapple Festival:** This October festival celebrates the local apple crop and scrapple, a fried pork mixture. Don't miss the scrapple-carving contest and the scrapple-toss event!

Snow geese at Bombay Hook National Wildlife Refuge

Georgetown

★ **Elsie Williams Doll Collection:**
This collection is a great way to
learn about customs and traditions
around the world. It features more
than 600 dolls from various countries, wearing traditional costumes
and special-occasion clothes.

★ **Trees of the States Arboretum:**
Do you know the official tree of
each state? You will after you take
a walking tour of this arboretum,
where you can see and read about
the state trees of all 50 states.
The arboretum is located on the
campus of Delaware Technical and
Community College.

★ **Treasures of the Sea:** This exhibit,
also on the college campus, features gold bars, cannons, and other
objects from a Spanish ship that
sank 400 years ago.

★ **Nutter D. Marvel Carriage
Museum:** Here you'll see 20
antique horse-drawn carriages.
Around the grounds is a collection
of local historic buildings, including barns, a school, a church, and a
blacksmith shop.

Lewes

★ **Cape Henlopen State Park:** Here
you can swim in the ocean, sun-
bathe and build sand castles on the
beach, or go hiking or biking along
the park's trails.

★ **Zwaanendael Museum:** Exhibits
tell the story of the Dutch people
who settled here in 1631. Other
displays highlight the area's military history and the explorers and
pirates who once cruised the coast.
At the museum, you can also see
riches recovered from a British
ship that sank 200 years ago.

SEE IT HERE!

GREAT DELAWARE KITE FESTIVAL

Thousands of kids of all ages enjoy the Great Delaware
Kite Festival. It's held in March or April at Cape Henlopen
State Park. Kids and adults compete in categories such
as best homemade kite, youngest and oldest flyer, and
highest flyer. Not everyone who attends flies kites. Some
people come to see the colorful kites fill the sky, while
others admire the stunt-kite flyers.

Seaford

★ **Eastern Shore AFRAM Festival:** This multicultural festival is held in Nutter Park every August. It celebrates African American heritage through music, dance, foods, and cultural exhibits.

Between Dewey Beach and Indian River Inlet

★ **Coin Beach:** Delawareans hunt for old coins along this stretch of beach, and you can, too! Coins from old shipwrecks often wash ashore here, especially after a storm.

★ **Indian River Life-Saving Station:** The guides at this historic lifesaving station, which was built to save victims of shipwrecks, tell thrilling tales of courageous rescues and haunting stories about the many shipwrecks that occurred along the coast.

Fenwick Island

★ **DiscoverSea Shipwreck Museum:** You'll marvel at thousands of artifacts recovered from shipwrecks, including jewelry, coins, weapons, and dishes. You'll also learn about shipwrecks along the Delaware coast and around the world.

Near Lowes Crossroads

★ **Cypress Swamp:** This wetland, partly in Trap Pond State Park, contains the most northerly natural grove of bald cypress trees in the country.

Milton

★ **Prime Hook National Wildlife Refuge:** This marshland provides nesting, feeding, and resting areas for waterbirds and shorebirds, especially when they're migrating. Here you'll see black ducks, wood ducks, black-necked stilts, snow geese, and many other bird species, along with lizards, turtles, and frogs.

Rehoboth Beach

★ **Boardwalk:** Stroll along the boardwalk for beautiful views of the ocean and the sandy beach. Then have some taffy or a funnel cake, or do some shopping at one of the hundreds of stores in town.

A crowd at Rehoboth Beach

WRITING PROJECTS

Check out these ideas for creating a campaign brochure and writing you-are-there narratives. Or research famous people from Delaware.

118

ART PROJECTS

You can illustrate the state song, create a dazzling PowerPoint presentation, or learn about the state quarter and design your own.

119

TIMELINE

What happened when? This timeline highlights important events in the state's history—and shows what was happening throughout the United States at the same time.

122

FAST FACTS

Use this section to find fascinating facts about state symbols, land area and population statistics, weather, sports teams, and much more.

126

GLOSSARY

Remember the Words to Know from the chapters in this book? They're all collected here.

125

SCIENCE, TECHNOLOGY, & MATH PROJECTS

Make weather maps, graph population statistics, and research endangered species that live in the state.

PRIMARY VS. SECONDARY SOURCES

So what are primary and secondary sources? And what's the diff? This section explains all that and where you can find them.

BIOGRAPHICAL DICTIONARY

This at-a-glance guide highlights some of the state's most important and influential people. Visit this section and read about their contributions to the state, the country, and the world.

RESOURCES

Books, Web sites, DVDs, and more. Take a look at these additional sources for information about the state.

WRITING PROJECTS

★ ★ ★

Write a Memoir, Journal, or Editorial for Your School Newspaper!
Picture Yourself . . .

★ Building a Lenape wigwam. Your family has just moved to a new riverside camp, so you join in to help build a wigwam for shelter. What materials would you use? Describe how you build the wigwam.

SEE: Chapter Two, pages 28–29.

GO TO: www.lenapelifeways.org/lenape2.htm

★ As a child working in a cannery in the 1880s. Describe what the cannery looks, smells, and feels like. Explain the process of canning food. What job do you do?

SEE: Chapter Four, page 53.

GO TO: www.intandem.com/NewPrideSite/MD/Lesson6/Lesson6_1.html

Create an Election Brochure or Web Site!

Run for office! Throughout this book, you've read about some of the issues that concern Delaware today. As a candidate for governor of Delaware, create a campaign brochure or Web site.

★ Explain how you meet the qualifications to be governor of Delaware.

★ Talk about the three or four major issues you'll focus on if you're elected.

★ Remember, you'll be responsible for Delaware's budget. How would you spend the taxpayers' money?

SEE: Chapter Seven, pages 90–92.

GO TO: Delaware's government Web site at www.delaware.gov. You might also want to read some local newspapers. Try these:

Dover Post at www.doverpost.com

News Journal at www.delawareonline.com

Create an interview script with a famous person from Delaware!

★ Research various Delawareans, such as Joseph Biden Jr., "Sugar Ray" Leonard, Annie Jump Cannon, Clifford Brown, or Caesar Rodney.

★ Based on your research, pick one person you would most like to talk with.

★ Write a script of the interview. What questions would you ask? How would this person answer? Create a question-and-answer format. You may want to supplement this writing project with a voice-recording dramatization of the interview.

SEE: Chapters Three, Four, Six, and Seven, pages 41, 55, 79, and 93, and the Biographical Dictionary, pages 133–136.

ART PROJECTS

★ ★ ★

Create a PowerPoint Presentation or Visitors' Guide

Welcome to Delaware!

Delaware is a great place to visit and to live! From its natural beauty to its historical sites, there's plenty to see and do. In your PowerPoint presentation or brochure, highlight 10 to 15 of Delaware's fascinating landmarks. Be sure to include:

★ a map of the state showing where these sites are located

★ photos, illustrations, Web links, natural history facts, geographic stats, climate and weather, plants and wildlife, and recent discoveries

SEE: Chapters One and Nine, pages 8–21 and 106–115.

GO TO: The official tourism Web site for Delaware at www.visitdelaware.com. Download and print maps, photos, and vacation ideas for tourists.

Illustrate the Lyrics to the Delaware State Song

("Our Delaware")

Use markers, paints, photos, collages, colored pencils, or computer graphics to illustrate the lyrics to "Our Delaware." Turn your illustrations into a picture book or scan them into PowerPoint and add music.

SEE: The lyrics to "Our Delaware" on page 128.

GO TO: The Delaware state government Web site at www.delaware.gov to find out more about the origin of the state song.

State Quarter Project

From 1999 to 2008, the U.S. Mint introduced new quarters commemorating each of the 50 states in the order that they were admitted to the Union. Each state's quarter features a unique design on its back, or reverse.

GO TO: www.usmint.gov/kids and find out what's featured on the back of the Delaware quarter.

★ Research the significance of the image. Who designed the quarter? Who chose the final design?

★ Design your own Delaware quarter. What images would you choose for the reverse?

★ Make a poster showing the Delaware quarter and label each image.

SCIENCE, TECHNOLOGY, & MATH PROJECTS

★ ★ ★

Graph Population Statistics!

★ Compare population statistics (such as ethnic background, birth, death, and literacy rates) in Delaware counties or major cities.

★ In your graph or chart, look at population density and write sentences describing what the population statistics show; graph one set of population statistics and write a paragraph explaining what the graphs reveal.

SEE: Chapter Six, pages 68–74.

GO TO: The official Web site for the U.S. Census Bureau at www.census.gov and at http://quickfacts.census.gov/qfd/states/10000.html, to find out more about population statistics, how they work, and what the statistics are for Delaware.

Create a Weather Map of Delaware!

Use your knowledge of Delaware's geography to research and identify conditions that result in specific weather events. What is it about the geography of Delaware that makes it vulnerable to things such as hurricanes? Create a weather map or poster that shows the weather patterns over the state. Include a caption explaining the technology used to measure weather phenomena such as hurricanes and provide data.

SEE: Chapter One, pages 15–16.

GO TO: The National Oceanic and Atmospheric Administration's National Weather Service Web site at www.weather.gov for weather maps and forecasts for Delaware.

Loggerhead turtle

Track Endangered Species

Using your knowledge of Delaware's wildlife, research which animals and plants are endangered or threatened.

★ Find out what the state is doing to protect these species.

★ Chart known populations of the animals and plants, and report on changes in certain geographic areas

SEE: Chapter One, pages 20–21.

GO TO: Web sites such as www.dnrec.state.de.us/fw/telist.htm for lists of endangered species in Delaware.

PRIMARY VS. SECONDARY SOURCES

★ ★ ★

What's the Diff?

Your teacher may require at least one or two primary sources and one or two secondary sources for your assignment. So, what's the difference between the two?

★ **Primary sources are original.** You are reading the actual words of someone's diary, journal, letter, autobiography, or interview. Primary sources can also be photographs, maps, prints, cartoons, news/film footage, posters, first-person newspaper articles, drawings, musical scores, and recordings. By the way, when you conduct a survey, interview someone, shoot a video, or take photographs to include in a project, you are creating primary sources!

★ **Secondary sources are what you find in encyclopedias, textbooks, articles, biographies, and almanacs.** These are written by a person or group of people who tell about something that happened to someone else. Secondary sources also recount what another person said or did. This book is an example of a secondary source.

Now that you know what primary sources are—where can you find them?

★ **Your school or local library:** Check the library catalog for collections of original writings, government documents, musical scores, and so on. Some of this material may be stored on microfilm. The Library of Congress Web site (www.loc.gov) is an excellent online resource for primary source materials.

★ **Historical societies:** These organizations keep historical documents, photographs, and other materials. Staff members can help you find what you are looking for. History museums are also great places to see primary sources firsthand.

★ **The Internet:** There are lots of sites that have primary sources you can download and use in a project or assignment.

TIMELINE

★ ★ ★

U.S. Events | 1400 | Delaware Events

1400s
Lenapes live in the Delaware River valley.

1492
Christopher Columbus and his crew sight land in the Caribbean Sea.

1500

1565
Spanish admiral Pedro Menéndez de Avilés founds St. Augustine, Florida, the oldest continuously occupied European settlement in the continental United States.

1600

Henry Hudson

1607
The first permanent English settlement in North America is established at Jamestown.

1609
Henry Hudson, an Englishman sailing for the Dutch East India Company, reaches Delaware Bay and River.

1610
English sea captain Samuel Argall names Delaware Bay and River after Lord De La Warr, the governor of Virginia.

1620
Pilgrims found Plymouth Colony, the second permanent English settlement.

1638
Swedish colonists establish Fort Christina, Delaware's first permanent European settlement, at present-day Wilmington.

William Penn addressing Swedish settlers

1664
Delaware becomes an English colony.

1682
René-Robert Cavelier, Sieur de La Salle, claims more than 1 million square miles (2.6 million sq km) of territory in the Mississippi River basin for France, naming it Louisiana.

1682
Englishman William Penn gains control of Delaware.

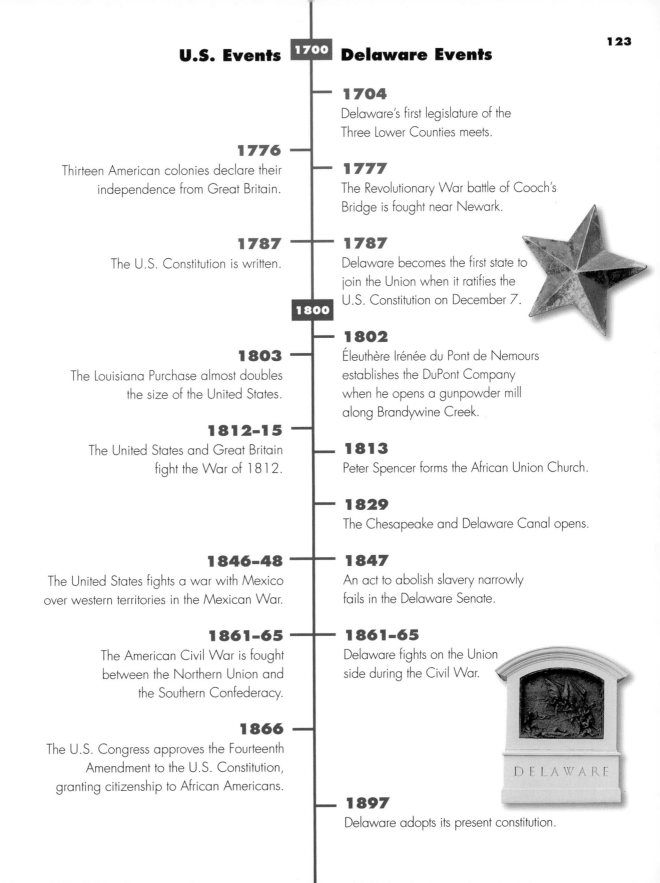

U.S. Events `1700` Delaware Events

1704
Delaware's first legislature of the
Three Lower Counties meets.

1776
Thirteen American colonies declare their
independence from Great Britain.

1777
The Revolutionary War battle of Cooch's
Bridge is fought near Newark.

1787
The U.S. Constitution is written.

1787
Delaware becomes the first state to
join the Union when it ratifies the
U.S. Constitution on December 7.

`1800`

1802
Éleuthère Irénée du Pont de Nemours
establishes the DuPont Company
when he opens a gunpowder mill
along Brandywine Creek.

1803
The Louisiana Purchase almost doubles
the size of the United States.

1812–15
The United States and Great Britain
fight the War of 1812.

1813
Peter Spencer forms the African Union Church.

1829
The Chesapeake and Delaware Canal opens.

1846–48
The United States fights a war with Mexico
over western territories in the Mexican War.

1847
An act to abolish slavery narrowly
fails in the Delaware Senate.

1861–65
The American Civil War is fought
between the Northern Union and
the Southern Confederacy.

1861–65
Delaware fights on the Union
side during the Civil War.

1866
The U.S. Congress approves the Fourteenth
Amendment to the U.S. Constitution,
granting citizenship to African Americans.

DELAWARE

1897
Delaware adopts its present constitution.

U.S. Events `1900` **Delaware Events**

1917–18
The United States engages in World War I.

1920
The Nineteenth Amendment to the U.S. Constitution grants women the right to vote.

1920
For the first time, more Delawareans live in urban areas than in rural areas.

1924
The DuPont Highway, the first highway to run through Delaware from north to south, opens.

1929
The stock market crashes, plunging the United States more deeply into the Great Depression.

1939
The DuPont Company opens the first nylon plant in Seaford.

1941–45
The United States engages in World War II.

1950
The University of Delaware begins admitting African American students.

1951–53
The United States engages in the Korean War.

1951
The Delaware Memorial Bridge opens, spanning the Delaware River and linking Delaware and New Jersey.

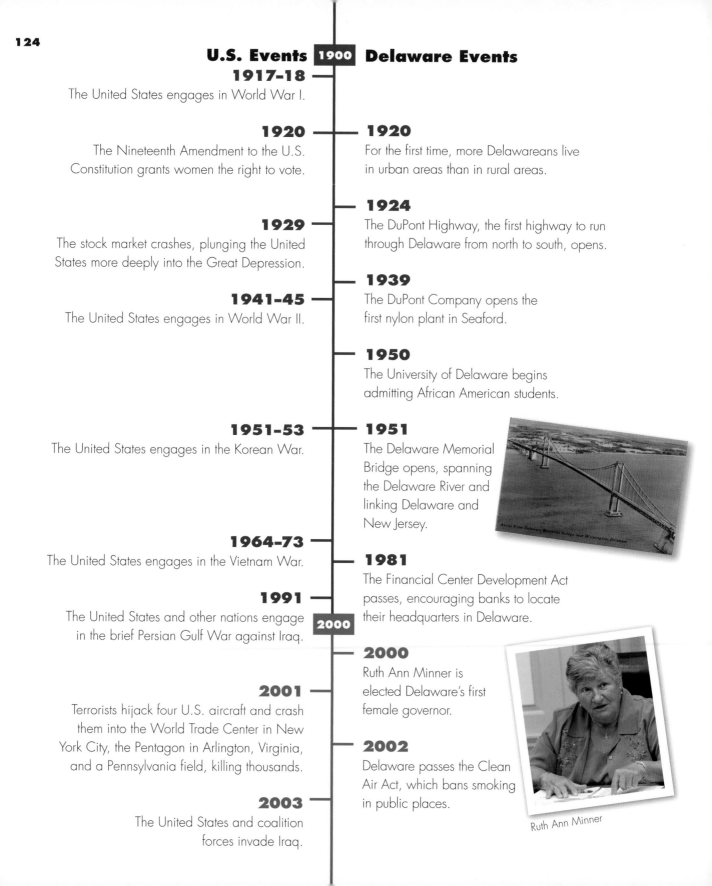

1964–73
The United States engages in the Vietnam War.

1981
The Financial Center Development Act passes, encouraging banks to locate their headquarters in Delaware.

1991
The United States and other nations engage in the brief Persian Gulf War against Iraq.

`2000`

2000
Ruth Ann Minner is elected Delaware's first female governor.

2001
Terrorists hijack four U.S. aircraft and crash them into the World Trade Center in New York City, the Pentagon in Arlington, Virginia, and a Pennsylvania field, killing thousands.

2002
Delaware passes the Clean Air Act, which bans smoking in public places.

2003
The United States and coalition forces invade Iraq.

Ruth Ann Minner

GLOSSARY

★ ★ ★

abolitionists people who work to end slavery

archaeologists people who study the remains of past human societies

canneries factories where food is canned

catapults machines with a long, wooden arm used to fling stones or other objects against or over walls

civil rights basic human rights that all citizens in a society are entitled to, such as the right to vote

colony a community settled in a new land but with ties to another government

discrimination unequal treatment based on race, gender, religion, or other factors

endangered in danger of becoming extinct

estuary the mouth of a river where the river's freshwater mixes with the salt water of the ocean, creating a variety of habitats

fugitives people who flee or escape

global warming the gradual warming of the entire planet brought about by increasing air pollution; some experts predict violent weather changes as one consequence

igneous describing rocks that have been created by magma and volcanic activity

incorporate to register as a company under the laws of a local, state, or national government

metamorphic describing rocks that have been changed by extreme pressure, wind, and water

nomadic describing someone who moves from place to place and does not permanently settle in one location

poll tax a fee a person must pay before he or she can vote

segregated separated from others according to race, class, ethnic group, religion, or other factors

synthetic artificial; related to something that doesn't occur in nature

terrapins turtles that live in fresh or slightly salty water

thoroughbred a horse carefully bred for generations to be a racing horse

threatened likely to become an endangered species in the foreseeable future

tributaries smaller rivers that flow into a larger river

whittling carving wood using only a small, light knife; usually done as a hobby

FAST FACTS

★ ★ ★

State Symbols

Statehood date	December 7, 1787; 1st state
Origin of state name	Named for Lord De La Warr, an early governor of Virginia. The name was originally applied to Delaware Bay and later to the Delaware River and to land that became the state.
State capital	Dover
State nicknames	The First State; Small Wonder; Diamond State
State motto	"Liberty and Independence"
State bird	Blue hen chicken
State flower	Peach blossom
State fish	Weakfish
State mineral	Sillimanite
State fruit	Peach
State butterfly	Tiger swallowtail
State fossil	Belemnite
State song	"Our Delaware" (See lyrics on page 128)
State tree	American holly
State bug	Ladybug
State beverage	Milk
State colors	Colonial blue and buff
State fair	Harrington, end of July

State seal

Geography

Total area; rank	2,489 square miles (6,446 sq km); 49th
Land; rank	1,954 square miles (5,061 sq km); 49th
Water; rank	536 square miles (1,388 sq km); 40th
Inland water; rank	72 square miles (186 sq km); 49th
Coastal water; rank	371 square miles (961 sq km); 15th
Territorial water; rank	93 square miles (241 sq km); 21st
Geographic center	Kent County, 11 miles (18 km) south of Dover
Latitude	38°27' N to 39°50' N
Longitude	75°2' W to 75°47' W

Highest point	451 feet (137 m), in New Castle County along the Pennsylvania state line
Lowest point	Sea level, along the coast
Largest city	Wilmington
Number of counties	3
Longest river	Delaware River

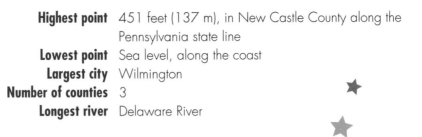

Population

Population; rank (2007 estimate)	864,764; 45th
Density (2007 estimate)	443 people per square mile (171 per sq km)
Population distribution (2000 census)	80% urban, 20% rural
Ethnic distribution (2007 estimate)	White persons: 74.5%*
	Black persons: 20.9%*
	Asian persons: 2.8%*
	American Indian and Alaska Native persons: 0.4%*
	Native Hawaiian and Other Pacific Islanders: 0.1%*
	Persons reporting two or more races: 1.4%
	Persons of Hispanic or Latino origin: 6.5%[†]
	White persons not Hispanic: 68.7%

Includes persons reporting only one race.
[†] Hispanics may be of any race, so they are also included in applicable race categories.

Weather

Record high temperature	110°F (43°C) at Millsboro on July 21, 1930
Record low temperature	−17°F (−27°C) at Millsboro on January 17, 1893
Average July temperature	77°F (25°C)
Average January temperature	32°F (0°C)
Average yearly precipitation	42 inches (107 cm)

State flag

STATE SONG

★ ★ ★

"Our Delaware"

Delaware's state song was adopted in 1925. Each of the first three verses honors one county. These verses were written by George B. Hynson. Donn Devine wrote an additional verse in praise of the state and its citizens' loyalty. Will M. S. Brown set the words to music.

Chorus:
Oh our Delaware! Our beloved Delaware!
For the sun is shining over our beloved
Delaware,
Oh our Delaware! Our beloved Delaware!
Here's the loyal son that pledges,
Faith to good old Delaware.

Oh the hills of dear New Castle,
and the smiling vales between,
When the corn is all in tassel,
And the meadowlands are green;
Where the cattle crop the clover,
And its breath is in the air,
While the sun is shining over
Our beloved Delaware.

(Chorus)

Where the wheat fields break and billow,
In the peaceful land of Kent,
Where the toiler seeks his pillow,
With the blessings of content;
Where the bloom that tints the peaches,
Cheeks of merry maidens share,
And the woodland chorus preaches
A rejoicing Delaware.

(Chorus)

Dear old Sussex visions linger,
Of the holly and the pine,
Of Henlopens Jeweled finger,
Flashing out across the brine;
Of the gardens and the hedges,
And the welcome waiting there,
For the loyal son that pledges
Faith to good old Delaware.

(Chorus)

From New Castle's rolling meadows,
Through the fair rich fields of Kent,
To the Sussex shores hear echoes,
Of the pledge we now present;
Liberty and Independence,
We will guard with loyal care,
And hold fast to freedom's presence,
In our home state Delaware.

NATURAL AREAS AND HISTORIC SITES

National Historic Trail

The *Captain John Smith Chesapeake National Historic Trail* is the nation's first national all-water trail. It follows the route of English colonist John Smith as he explored the Chesapeake Bay area between 1607 and 1609.

State Parks and Forests

Delaware's state park system maintains 16 state park and recreation areas, including *Brandywine Creek State Park*, which was a dairy farm owned by the du Pont family before becoming a state park in 1965. It contains the first two nature preserves in Delaware. It also includes 14 miles (23 km) of trails.

Another beautiful and historic state park is *Fort Delaware State Park*, located on Pea Patch Island. Union troops used the fort as a prison for Confederate soldiers captured in battle during the Civil War. Today, the park is accessible only by ferry.

Other Delaware state parks include *Trap Pond State Park*, which is one of the largest surviving fragments of an extensive patch of second-growth bald cypress trees, and *White Clay Creek State Park*.

Bird-watchers at Brandywine Creek State Park

SPORTS TEAMS

★ ★ ★

NCAA Teams (Division I)

Delaware State University *Hornets*
University of Delaware *Fightin' Blue Hens*

A University of Delaware player tries to shake off a tackle during a matchup with the University of Massachusetts.

CULTURAL INSTITUTIONS

Libraries

Delaware State Archives (Dover) and the Delaware State Historical Society (Wilmington) both have fine collections on Delaware history.

The *Eleutherian Mills-Hagley Foundation* (Greenville) has a noted collection on American economic history.

The *University of Delaware Library* (Newark) has a highly regarded collection on Delaware's history, as well as a 2,000-volume collection of books on the public and private life of Abraham Lincoln.

Museums

The *Delaware Archaeology Museum* (Dover) encompasses 12,000 years of Delaware's archaeological history.

The *Hagley Museum* (Wilmington) offers exhibits featuring industrial life in the 1800s.

Nanticoke Indian Museum (Millsboro) is located in what was once a one-room schoolhouse for Nanticoke children. The museum explores jewelry, pottery, tools, and other items made by Delaware's Nanticoke people.

The *Winterthur Museum and Country Estate* (Wilmington) is the former home of Henry Francis du Pont, an American antiques collector. The museum's collection includes American decorative arts made or used from 1640 to 1860. The estate's garden, spread over nearly 1,000 acres (405 ha), has ponds, woods, meadowlands, and both native and nonnative plants.

Zwaanendael Museum (Lewes) commemorates Delaware's first European colony, Zwaanendael, established by the Dutch in 1631. It serves as a showcase for Lewes-area maritime, military, and social history.

Performing Arts

Delaware has one major opera company and one major orchestra.

Universities and Colleges

In 2006, Delaware had five public and four private institutions of higher learning.

ANNUAL EVENTS

January–March

Yuletide at Winterthur (January)

Delaware Home & Garden Show (March)

Great Delaware Kite Festival at Cape Henlopen State Park (March or April)

April–June

Boardwalk Fashion Promenade at Rehoboth Beach (Easter Sunday)

Irish Festival at Hagley Museum near Wilmington (last Saturday in April)

Old Dover Days (first Saturday in May)

Wilmington Garden Day (first Saturday in May)

Winterthur Point-to-Point Horse Race (first Sunday in May)

A Day in Old New Castle (May)

Greek Festival and Italian Festival in Wilmington (June)

July–September

Delaware State Fair in Harrington (July)

Rockwood's Victorian Ice Cream Festival in Wilmington (July)

Bethany Beach Boardwalk Arts Festival (August)

Nanticoke Indian Powwow in Millsboro (second week in September)

Brandywine Arts Festival in Wilmington (second Saturday in September)

Dover 400 NASCAR Race (September)

October–December

Fall Harvest Festival at the Delaware Agricultural Museum in Dover (late October)

World Championship Punkin Chunkin in Millsboro (November)

Candlelight tours of historic homes in New Castle (December)

Christmas and candlelight tours at nine museums in the Brandywine Valley (December)

The Delaware State Fair

BIOGRAPHICAL DICTIONARY

Richard Allen (1760–1831) was born into slavery but was freed as a young man. He became a minister and formed the African Methodist Episcopal Church in 1816. He grew up in Dover.

Valerie Bertinelli (1960–) is an actress best known for her role as Barbara Cooper on the TV series *One Day at a Time*. She was born in Wilmington and grew up in Claymont.

Joseph Biden Jr. See page 93.

Robert Montgomery Bird (1806–1854) was a doctor and artist who wrote plays and historical novels. He was born in New Castle.

Emily Bissell (1861–1948) was a social worker and activist. She introduced special stamps called Christmas Seals to raise funds to fight tuberculosis, a deadly lung disease. She was born in Wilmington.

Clifford Brown (1930–1956) was a jazz trumpet player. His style, known for its speed and precision, influenced many other musicians of his time. He was born in Wilmington.

Ken Burns (1953–) is a filmmaker who has produced documentaries such as *The Civil War*, *Baseball*, and *Jazz*. He spent several years of his childhood in Newark.

Henry S. Canby (1878–1961) was an editor and author. His book *The Brandywine* tells of the history along this Delaware river. He was born in Wilmington.

Annie Jump Cannon See page 55.

Wallace Carothers See page 104.

Mary Ann Shadd Cary See page 51.

Christopher Castellani (1972–) is a novelist who highlights Italian culture. For his novel *The Saint of Lost Things*, he drew on his childhood memories as the son of Italian immigrants in Wilmington.

Robert Crumb (1943–), usually known as just R. Crumb, is a comic book cartoonist. He created many popular comics in the 1960s. He lived in Milford as a teenager.

Felix Darley (1821–1888) was an artist who illustrated books by authors such as Charles Dickens and Washington Irving. Darley's mansion in Claymont is now a historic site.

John Dickinson See page 41.

Éleuthère Irénée (E. I.) du Pont de Nemours (1771–1834) was a chemist and industrialist. He founded the gunpowder mill that grew into the DuPont Company, one of the largest chemical companies in the world. Born in France, he built the family home at Eleutherian Mills near Greenville.

Ken Burns

Valerie Bertinelli

Henry Francis du Pont (1880–1969) was an art collector whose home and art collection formed the basis of the Winterthur Museum and Country Estate near Greenville.

Oliver Evans (1755–1819) was the inventor of machines for carding wool and milling grain, as well as several types of steam engines. He was born near Newport.

Yvette Freeman (1957–) is an actress who appeared in the TV series *ER*. She was born in Wilmington.

Thomas Garrett See page 50.

Dallas Green (1934–) is a former manager of the Philadelphia Phillies, New York Yankees, and New York Mets baseball teams. He was born in Newport.

Henry Heimlich (1920–) is a surgeon who invented the Heimlich maneuver, a procedure to save choking victims. He was born in Wilmington.

Gilbert "Cisco" Houston (1918–1961) was a folksinger who sang cowboy ballads, railroad songs, and laborers' songs. He often performed with folksinger Woody Guthrie. Houston was born in Wilmington.

Yvette Freeman

John Hunn (1818–1894) was an abolitionist who helped thousands of people escape to freedom on the Underground Railroad. He was born in Kent County and lived in Odessa.

Eldridge Johnson (1867–1945) was the inventor of the motorized phonograph record player and the founder of the Victor Talking Machine Company. He was born in Wilmington.

William "Judy" Johnson See page 85.

Patrick Kerr (1956–) is an actor who appeared in the TV comedy *Frasier*. He was born in Wilmington.

Ray Charles "Sugar Ray" Leonard (1956–) is a retired boxer. He won a gold medal at the 1976 Olympics, as well as several world championships. He was born in Wilmington.

John P. Marquand (1893–1960) was a novelist who won the 1938 Pulitzer Prize for fiction for *The Late George Apley*. He also created the Mr. Moto spy series. He was born in Wilmington.

"Sugar Ray" Leonard

Kevin Mench (1978–) is a baseball player. Born in Wilmington, he played for the University of Delaware Fightin' Blue Hens. He went on to play outfield for the Texas Rangers and the Milwaukee Brewers.

Ruth Ann Minner See page 90.

Joseph Miró See page 92.

Robert Mitchum (1917–1997) was an actor who appeared in more than 100 movies. He spent part of his childhood in Felton.

Russell Peterson See page 21.

Ryan Phillippe (1974–) is an actor who has appeared in movies such as *Breach* and *Flags of Our Fathers*. He was born in New Castle.

Teri Polo (1969–) is an actress who has starred in the TV shows *The West Wing* and *Northern Exposure* and in films such as *Meet the Parents*. She was born in Dover.

Howard Pyle See page 78.

George Read (1733–1798) was a signer of the Declaration of Independence. He also served as chief justice of Delaware, a U.S. senator, a member of the Continental Congress, and president (governor) of Delaware. Born in Maryland, he lived most of his life in New Castle.

Kevin Mench

Teri Polo

Louis Redding See page 61.

Judge Reinhold (1957–) is an actor whose movies include *My Brother the Pig* and the Santa Clause movies. He was born in Wilmington as Edward Ernest Reinhold.

Caesar Rodney (1728–1784) was a signer of the Declaration of Independence, a member of the Continental Congress, and a governor of Delaware. He was born in Dover.

Mark E. Rogers (1952–) is an artist and author who wrote and illustrated the Samurai Cat books. He lives in Newark.

Cynthia Rothrock (1957–) is a martial arts champion who has appeared in dozens of martial arts movies. She holds black belts in five Korean and Chinese martial arts styles and is a five-time World Karate champion. She was born in Wilmington.

Elizabeth Shue (1963–) is an actress whose movies include *The Karate Kid*, *Back to the Future Part II*, *Back to the Future Part III*, and *Gracie*. She was born in Wilmington.

Peter Spencer See page 49.

Susan Stroman (1954–) is a Tony Award–winning choreographer for many Broadway musical shows, including *Show Boat* and *The Producers*, which she also directed. She was born in Wilmington.

Helen Thomas (1921–) is a women's rights activist. She helped organize the Delaware chapter of the National Organization for Women in 1970.

Sean Patrick Thomas (1970–) is an actor who starred in the movie *Save the Last Dance* and the TV series *The District*. He was born in Wilmington.

George Thorogood (1950–) is a blues and rock singer and songwriter. His band, the Destroyers, is sometimes called the Delaware Destroyers. He was born in Naamans Gardens, a suburb of Wilmington.

George Alfred Townsend (1841–1914) was a newspaper journalist who reported on the Civil War. As a novelist, his best-known work is *The Entailed Hat*. He was born in Georgetown.

Sean Patrick Thomas

Elizabeth Traynor (?–) is an artist and an illustrator for books and magazines. The first children's book she illustrated was *F Is for First State: A Delaware Alphabet*. She grew up in Delaware and began her art training at the Delaware Art Museum.

Johnny Weir (1984–) is a figure skater. He began skating at age 12 and moved to Delaware to train. He was the U.S. skating champion in 2004, 2005, and 2006.

Andrew Wyeth (1917–) is an artist. He is sometimes called the Painter of the People because his work is so popular. Many of his subjects are scenes in the Brandywine Valley.

Jamie Wyeth (1946–) is an artist. Many of his paintings feature birds, such as gulls, crows, and chickens. Born in Wilmington, he is the son of Andrew Wyeth and the grandson of N. C. Wyeth.

N. C. Wyeth (1882–1945) was an artist and one of the country's finest book illustrators. He studied art with Howard Pyle in Wilmington from 1902 to 1904.

Lara M. Zeises See page 80.

George Thorogood

RESOURCES

BOOKS

Nonfiction

Billus, Kathleen. *Judy Johnson*. New York: Rosen Central, 2002.

Levine, Michelle. *The Delaware*. Minneapolis: Lerner, 2007.

Melchiore, Susan McCarthy. *Caesar Rodney: American Patriot*. Philadelphia: Chelsea House Publishers, 2000.

Moose, Katie. *Uniquely Delaware*. Chicago: Heinemann Library, 2004.

Raymond, Aaron. *A Primary Source History of the Colony of Delaware*. New York: Rosen Central, 2006.

Worth, Richard. *Delaware* (Life in the Thirteen Colonies). Danbury, Conn.: Children's Press, 2004.

Fiction

Anderson, M. T., and Kurt Cyrus (illustrator). *Jasper Dash and the Flame-Pits of Delaware*. New York: Harcourt Children's Books, 2008.

Hesse, Karen. *A Light in the Storm: The Civil War Diary of Amelia Martin, Fenwick Island, Delaware 1861*. New York: Scholastic, 2003.

Zeises, Lara M. *Bringing Up the Bones*. New York: Delacorte Press, 2002.

DVDs

Discoveries . . . America: Delaware. Bennett-Watt Entertainment, 2004.

Protecting Our Water: Who's Got the Power? Delaware Nature Society, 1998.

WEB SITES AND ORGANIZATIONS

Black Americans in Delaware: An Overview
www.udel.edu/BlackHistory/overview.html
Visit this site to learn more about the history of African Americans in the state.

Delaware Department of Transportation: Archaeology
www.deldot.gov/archaeology/arch_intro.shtml
Learn more about Delaware's early residents.

Delaware Historical Society
www.hsd.org
You can find more details about Delaware's history at this site.

Delaware Tourism Office
www.visitdelaware.com
Go to this site for information about vacationing in Delaware.

State of Delaware Kids Page
www.state.de.us/gic/kidspage
For homework help, you can visit this site for information on things to see and do in Delaware. It also has links to other kids' sites.

State of Delaware: The Official Website for the First State
www.delaware.gov
For information on state government, history, facts, and recreation, visit this site.

INDEX

★ ★ ★

AUTHOR'S TIPS AND SOURCE NOTES

★   ★   ★

While writing this book, I consulted a number of sources, both online and at the library. For details about Delaware's earliest cultures, I found a wealth of information on the State Historic Preservation Office's Web site (www.destatemuseums.org/archaeology/points/prehist.shtml). The Delaware Historical Society's Web site, *Delaware History Explorer Online Encyclopedia* (www.hsd.org/DHE/DHE_welcome.htm), provides great articles on the people, places, and events in Delaware's history. For interesting places to visit, the best site is the state government's official visitor's guide at www.visitdelaware.com. It divides places into categories such as history and heritage, arts and culture, and outdoor recreation, so you can easily find what interests you.

Many good books shed light on Delaware's history and culture. Among the best is *History of Delaware*, by John A. Munroe. It provides an in-depth look at Delaware, from colonial times through the formation of the state, the Great Depression, the civil rights movement, and modern concerns. Another good history survey is *Delaware: A Bicentennial History*, by Carol Hoffecker. It gives a detailed overview of the state's history from early times to the 20th century. Hoffecker, a retired University of Delaware history professor, has written many other books on the state's history.